SIX YEARS AFTER
D-DAY

To Rose Mary —
Try it sometime!
Marie Bennett Alsmeyer
June / 1995

SIX YEARS AFTER
D-DAY

Cycling through Europe

Marie Bennett Alsmeyer

Introduction by Linda Grant De Pauw

University of North Texas Press
Denton, Texas

First Edition 1995

10 9 8 7 6 5 4 3 2 1

The paper in this book meets the minimum requirements of the
American National Standard for Permanence of paper for Printed
Library Materials, Z39.48- 1984.

Library of Congress Cataloging-in-Publication Data

Alsmeyer, Marie Bennett.
Six years after D-Day: cycling through Europe / Marie Bennett
Alsmeyer.
p.   cm.
Includes index.
ISBN 0-929398-82-3
1. Europe—Description and travel. 2. Alsmeyer, Marie Bennett—
Journeys—Europe. I. Title.

D921.A48   1995   94-48004
914.04'555—dc20   CIP

Cover and interior design
by Amy Layton

All photographs provided by
Hank and Marie Bennett Alsmeyer

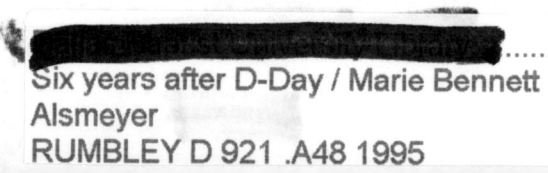

Table of Contents

Acknowledgments

This book is written in loving memory of Mary Grillet of Draveil, France, who, with her family, encouraged us to leave South Texas and see what the rest of the world was all about.

I am also indebted to my husband, Henry, who corrected sentence structure and errors in subject-verb agreement in addition to keeping a watchful eye upon *The Chicago Manual of Style*. But more especially, I will be forever grateful for his unending "routes et grandes curiositiés" for those roads less traveled.

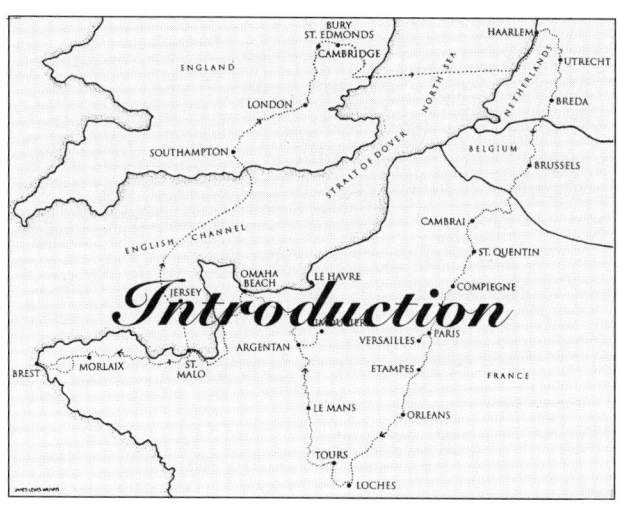

The movement to recover the military history of women who served in World War II owes a great deal to Marie Bennett Alsmeyer. Forty years after her service, she published her classic memoir, *The Way of the WAVES* (Conway, Arkansas: Hamba Books, 1981). Although two WAVES had published books during the war years, Alsmeyer was the first Navy enlisted woman to write as a veteran. She did not tell her story publicly until forty years after she entered the military.

Today we wonder at the long silence during which women veterans of the greatest war in history were invisible and forgotten. Military service is not just for men anymore. Rigid gender distinctions have faded as Navy women fly combat missions over Iraq and a woman captain commands the Star Trek starship *Voyager* in the world of popular fantasy. Yet as recently as fifteen years ago, when Alsmeyer's pioneering volume appeared, most women who had served in uniform hesitated to identify themselves publicly as veterans. Whatever official pronouncements by recruiters might be, the whispers were that any woman in the military was either a prostitute or a lesbian.

But Marie Alsmeyer was and is a lady with a naturally sunny disposition, secure in the approval and support of family and friends. She was always proud to have served, used her GI bill benefits to attend the university where she met her husband, and considered herself to be as much a veteran as he was. She shared with other well-brought-up girls of her era, the ability to avoid, ignore, misunderstand or make a joke of nasty innuendos or what would today be called sexual harassment. With the charming innocence that shines through her writing, she originally intended to call her memoir *The Making of a WAVE*. Her husband told her she absolutely must not use that title. She saw nothing wrong with it; in *Books in Print* there were listings for *The Making of a Surgeon*, *The Making of a Politician*, and dozens more. Nevertheless, she bowed to his opinion.

In 1981 no publisher was interested in her manuscript; indeed, even today, the memoirs of military women are difficult to place with established presses. Fortunately, Alsmeyer's husband, a former newspaperman and librarian, encouraged her to self-publish and contributed his professional expertise. The book was received enthusiastically by other women who had served in the Navy during World War II. They wrote her fan mail and included their own stories. A year after publication of her first book, Alsmeyer published a second volume: *Old WAVES Tales* (Conway, Arkansas: Hamba Books, 1982) based on these letters.

Before our own time, the histories of women in war have faded from memory with the generation that witnessed the events. Stories shared with family and friends at private gatherings or veterans' conventions live only as long as the narrators. Books published in limited editions, which do not find a place on the shelves of major libraries, become rare collectors' items or are permanently lost. Today, women realize that their stories are part of history too. Scholars now take women's military history seriously, thus encouraging both the production and preservation of memoirs.

Memoirs must be produced before they can be preserved. The World War II generation will not be with us much longer. By giving us another book, *Six Years After D-Day: Cycling Through Europe*, Alsmeyer provides inspiration and sets a splendid example for all older women, not just veterans this time, but every woman who has lived long enough to have a sense of her own history. Alsmeyer's joy in writing, the pleasure she finds in actively recalling and recreating the past in memory and then in words, shines through every page.

"I never would have imagined it possible to feel the past reaching right into the present and to know I was connected beyond all distances and time by a mere box of forgotten letters and journals," Alsmeyer writes. "When I pause in idleness, it is not in an effort of recalling, but the pleasure of reliving an indulgence of the senses." And again, "I look forward to writing time as if it were a reward. It is the best time of the day."

Besides her "box of memories" that brings back the sights, sounds and smells of the past, the ingredients for Alsmeyer's writing are "a ream of paper and a floppy disk." Her reference to modern technology reminds us that the physical effort of writing is less than it once was. No longer must a writer strive to create a clean copy with a dip pen and an inkwell or on a hunt-and-peck typewriter with carbon paper. We can hope that many, many women who enjoy reading this book will come to the last page and then dig out their own boxes of memorabilia, recall the adventures of their lives and tell their stories, and that younger readers will seek out their older relatives and ask them to remember what life was like for them fifty years ago.

Linda Grant De Pauw
Founder and President
The MINERVA Center
Pasadena, Maryland 21122

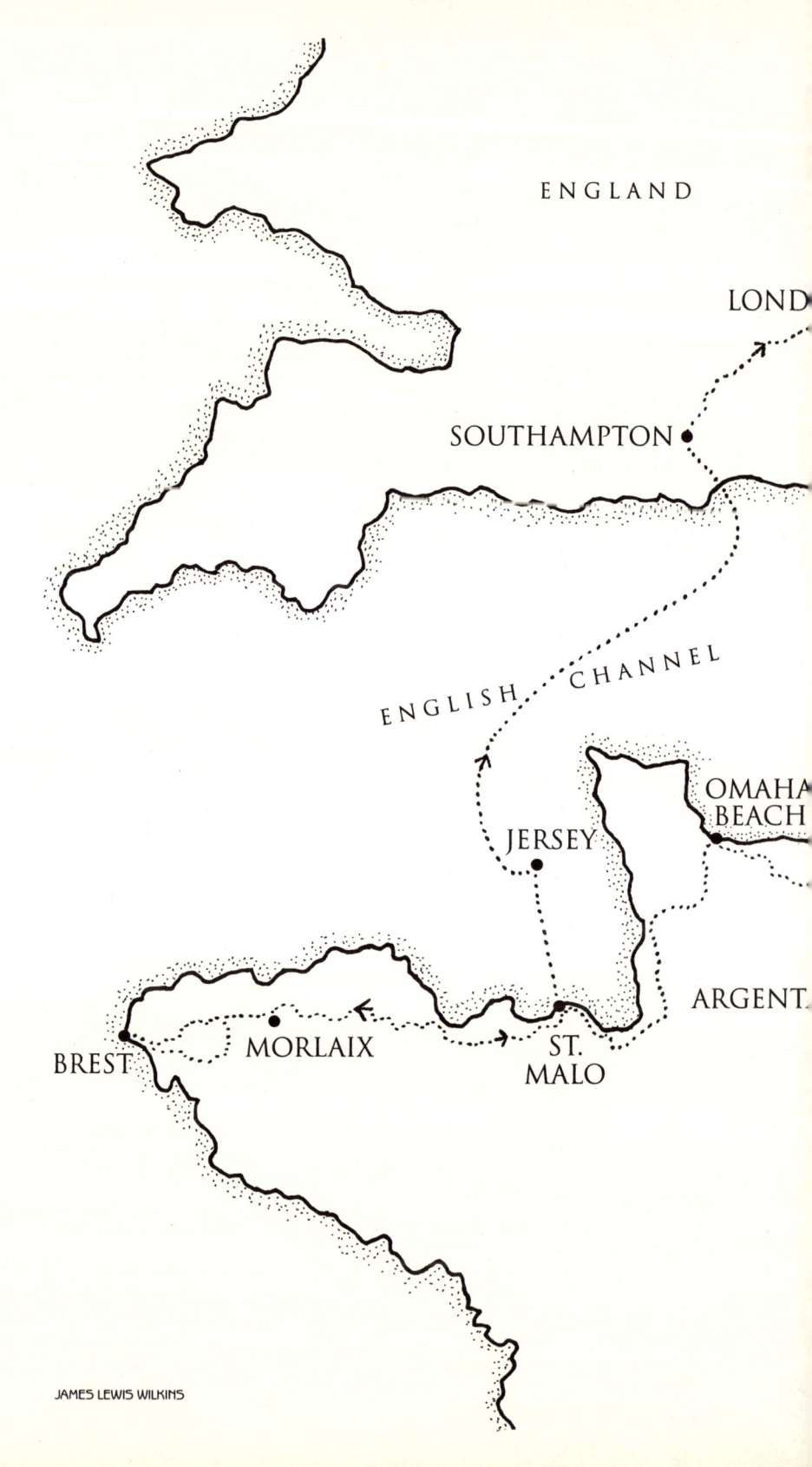

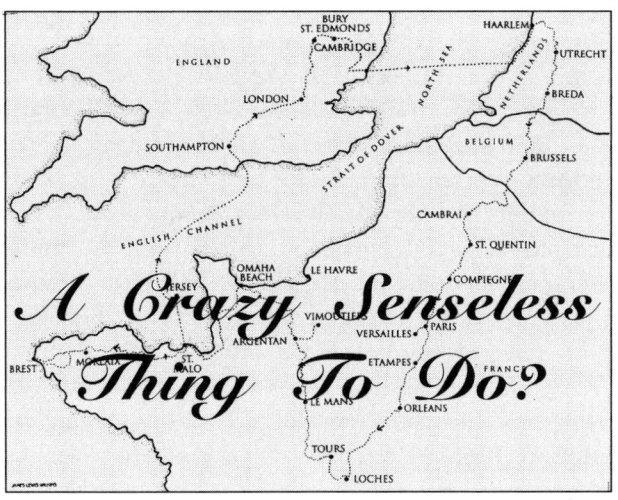

$\mathcal{B}$icycling more than 1200 miles through the Loire Valley, Normandy and Brittany in France, crossing to Southampton and back through the Hook of Holland to Paris makes no sense. True. But in 1950, it was a gloriously, magnificently, wondrously, and beautifully crazy senseless thing to do.

"It is something I am ready to do all over again," I tell our grown children as we sit around the kitchen table drinking coffee and eating warm sourdough bread.

"At *your* age?" Ann gasps.

"At *my* age? At what age do you consider someone 'old'? It's not as bad as I was led to believe."

The past, the memories—realities brought back suddenly by a scent, the shape of a hill, a rainbow—some triviality—still makes me suddenly say "I remember when. . . ." This is one of the compensations that age brings. To remember. And why not? Ann raises her eyebrows and gives her brothers a questioning look. Why would their mother, after more than forty-five years of a perfectly content

1

married life in Texas, want to cycle again through winding cobbled streets of Europe?

Actually, this thought came to me after David gave me a small paperback book, *Fat Man on a Bicycle.* Tom Vernon from Muswell Hill near London wrote a humorous book about pedaling his nineteen-stone body—that's 266 pounds American weight—through France to the Mediterranean as part of a BBC Radio 4 Programme. Vernon weighed even more when he wrote a second book about cycling the famous Roman Road. If an Englishman shaped like a cuddly teddy bear can still pedal his two-wheeler, why can't a little gray-haired tennis playing grandmother do the same?

During the Great Depression, the future for most young women was to become a secretary, nurse, teacher—or get married and have children. That suddenly changed with the outbreak of World War II. I quit my job with the War Price and Rationing Board, enlisted as a Navy WAVE and was assigned as a hospital corpsman at a Naval Receiving Hospital on the West Coast. It was like being at the end of a pendulum, suspended from a fixed point but swinging freely from that part of my life in a small Texas town to a tiny speck lost among thousands of sailors. Suddenly I was changed from a very frightened wide-eyed girl in sturdy black oxfords into a real person. After V-J Day, thanks to the GI Bill's tuition, books and $75 a month, I received a journalism degree from The University of Texas and met my future husband, Hank.

We literally lived on a shoestring, but I was determined we would not to fall into the same rut as some of our friends. It might have been an idiotic thing to do, but we quit work and with little money, booked passage to Europe on a French freighter. Unscheduled erratic sailing dates, changed itineraries and cycling miles over rough cobblestones didn't faze us. Until I recently unpacked a box of faded letters and journals that my mother had carefully stored away, I had forgotten what a wonderful summer it was.

It began on April Fools' Day 1950. Would I do it all over again? Of course! The children sit around the table—speechless, just like our parents four decades earlier. I try to convince them that life was much less complicated before television, computers and microwave ovens.

Bicycles were heavier and did not have fancy gear shifts and pull brakes, toe clips or twelve-inch tooth sprockets designed for what they describe as the "average male." Women's bicycles were

*Marie Bennett Alsmeyer and her husband Hank, studying
maps in preparation for their cycling trip.*

the same as men's, only smaller and without crossbars. Today's
cyclists wear flashy fluorescent Lycra spandex pants, helmets and
leather gloves. I can't picture Hank's tall thin body in anything but
his khakis and GI field jacket, and I wore skirts and sweaters, not
shorts or slacks.

I do not suggest our 1950 bicycle venture was anything like
today's "Tour de France" where men cycle 2500 miles wearing
aerodynamic helmets and riding streamlined bikes with tri-athlete
handlebars. It would not even be similar to the annual "Hotter'n
Hell" hundred-mile race in North Texas. This time, I would like to
cycle slowly, not over mountains and cobblestones, but through
softly rolling hills of East Anglia with a gentle breeze at my back.

Convincing our children it would be a wonderfully senseless
and crazy adventure is no easy task, even though I tell them their
parents have not always been on Medicare. They have no reason to
be shocked that forty-five years ago we, too, were young. We found

the Folies Bergères much more risque than the opera *Faust* and, needless to say, we enjoyed it more. This "aging syndrome" is all relative and I am not ready for it yet.

"Why don't you ride your little blue bicycle around here in East Texas?" Ann finally asks, even though she seems to feel cycling leaves much to be desired. "If the fat man from London cycled to the south of France and later traced England's ancient Roman Roads, you could easily make your way along El Camino Real where Spaniards crossed Texas three centuries ago."

"El Camino Real. King's Highway. Old Spanish Road. Old San Antonio Road. Call it what you like, it's still Texas Highway 21. The distance from the Rio Grande to the Sabine River is about 600 miles, almost the same as traveling from Southampton to Edinburgh," David added. "Why don't you stay here in Texas?"

"It wouldn't be the same, David!" Charles insisted. "East Anglia isn't anything like Texas. We've got sandy cow trails lined with mesquite and cactus; they've got lovely rolling hills. Tortillas and goat cheese wouldn't taste like crusty french bread and Camembert!"

"They both sound rather interesting, however," I answer, looking at Ann. She gave me that "Oh mom!" look.

"Call it RE-cycling!" suggested Charles. "I think you should go for it. For your own enjoyment, if nothing else! I'd like to see your Michelin maps again. I can't imagine what a trip like that would cost today. Remember, Mom, the book by Arthur Frommer on traveling Europe on $5 a day has been out of print for years."

"You have quit teasing and gone to meddlin' now," I told them. "Besides, Frommer wrote his book on how to save money seven years *after* we bicycled through Europe."

How quickly memories of the spring and summer of 1950 came back to life. It was something like living on the edge, with complete freedom to explore. Hank and I often saw things differently. And still do, fortunately. Hank, the perfectionist, navigated us safely and surely through mountains and rugged back roads, guided not by a brilliant star, but a handful of Michelin maps. His maps seemed to alert him to the rivers, mountain ranges and precisely how many kilometers there were between tiny villages—where one area ends and another begins. He noted carefully in his journal each day's weather, and mentally changed our crisp United States dollars into francs and pounds and guilders.

Detailed maps meant nothing to me, however. The most valuable thing my mother taught me was that it is all right not to understand all those wiggly lines. People who understand road maps, she insisted, are engaged in the lowest form of cunning. Therefore, I thought it was all right that I liked chasing rainbows across rain-soaked fields and absorbing the aroma of damp fresh mowed grass more than keeping my nose pressed to a map. I told him then, and continue to tell him now, that maps have no soul. He still disagrees.

I turn to Hank sitting quietly at the end of the table smoking his pipe. "Remember the B&B in London?"

He smiles but makes no comment.

"Remind me to tell you Mrs. Philips' wartime story about frying an egg, 'itler or no 'itler during a London buzz bomb raid," I say to the children.

There is very little similarity between our bicycle jaunt in 1950 and that of the Fat Man who traveled thirty years later. He wrote that he left his wife, two sons and a lazy cat in his creaky Edwardian house while he traveled first class across France, making a BBC Radio 4 series. Jenny, a BBC Radio correspondent from London, followed him in her car, which was loaded with cameras and tape recorders. She brought the pudgy cyclist gourmet lunches of fresh ham on warm baked bread with fancy cheese. He sipped expensive wine while resting beneath shady roadside trees. Vernon's hotel reservations were prearranged, Jenny making sure important people along the way were out to greet him. Still, the Englishman may have been overweight and overstaffed, but his book is a wonderfully genial reminder that no one is too fat—or too old—to bicycle in the chilly north of France, over the rolling hills of England or the polders of Holland.

It was quite different for us. While we cycled in Europe, most of our possessions, including the ironing board, were stored in our old 1940 Ford coupe parked in the alley behind Hank's grandmother's house in South Texas. We bought the cheapest cheese and bread we could find in local markets and drank very inexpensive dry wine as we picnicked on Hank's field jacket. Each road seemed to lead from one historic site to another, from one medieval village to the next, as if we were making a pilgrimage into ancient times.

Things themselves are not important, but the days spent going through a box of letters and journals, renewing those memories of cycling through Europe, are more than mere possessions. They are the keys to reopening long-neglected secret adventures. When I use the word "was," it seems to fix things in the past. But this isn't about the past, it is very much about the present. Hank and I were young, energetic, and filled with anticipation. Aboard the *Pont L'Evêque*, I didn't know what to expect, but was confident our journey would present an exciting challenge.

The challenge now is to go beyond thinking that things had to have happened a certain way in order for our lives to be as they are today. As I write, I am able to linger when I want, to jump backwards and forwards as I wish. For no reason that makes sense, the letters and notes I wrote long ago remind me today of many other events not on the pages, things I have not thought of for decades. The past suddenly crowds out the present and although I don't expect to be able to keep up chronological continuity, I can at least try to begin at the beginning.

"Re-cycle?" I say to my children. "Why not?"

No one says a word.

*H*ank first met Mary Grillet at the British Methodist Church in Paris after he was sent to Orly Field in 1945. Like many American servicemen who were welcomed into homes of the French people after the war, the tall thin sergeant was called "Tex" and literally claimed as one of the Grillet family. Hank has told me many stories about M. and Mme. Grillet and their three children, who all lived in Draveil, a village only a few kilometers from Paris. Mary had grown up near Shrewsbury in Shropshire, an English county bordering southern Wales. Sometime after their marriage, they moved to Draveil where Mary began teaching English in the local schools. She took her pupils to England for a week or so during the summers, and in her spare time she would entertain foreign students. During the worst days of World War II, as the Germans tried to take over Paris, she and the children did not remain in Draveil, but took shelter in a friend's tent in Les Ormes in the Loire Valley.

"Come visit us this spring," Mary had insisted. "Leave your luggage in Draveil and bicycle around."

7

"Why not?" I had asked Hank one wintry night a few months after we were married. "What have we got to lose? We have no money, but no debts either. We are not responsible to anyone. Why not?" The thought of cycling around Europe soon became more of a reality, and we began checking maps and sailing dates. We did not think of finances until later.

It was with great excitement that we opened Mary's letter a few weeks before we were to sail. "Chère Marie. Cher Tex," she wrote. "Merci de vos bonnes lettres—apprenez bien le français avec le 2nd mail." Luckily, the rest of her letter was written in English. She promised to meet us at a Paris train terminal—no matter what the hour—and to make reservations for us at a clean, inexpensive hotel in a quiet district. Railway fares to Draveil were 300 francs, return Juvisy for two, she wrote. She urged us to see as much of Paris as possible before beginning our bicycling. Her son Jean said that a new bicycle would cost about 14,000 francs.

Everything finally began to fall into place. Hank was earning $55 a week as a reporter for a weekly newspaper in South Texas, and I was paid even less as secretary in the dean's office of a nearby college. We lived in a one-room garage apartment with a pull-down bed. Our transportation was "Mrs. Riley," a prewar Ford coupe we jokingly named after the original owner, the local seamstress and buttonhole maker. Reservations on a French freighter from New Orleans to Le Havre had been confirmed and the GI Bill would allot $150 for six weeks tuition at the University in Fribourg, where we planned to enroll for summer classes after taking our bicycle tour. Hank carefully noted in his journal that on March 24, 1950, a week before we were to sail, he withdrew most of our assets—$535.50—from the bank, leaving only enough for return fare in September.

To earn a little money freelancing, Hank wrote a feature about South Texas snakes and received $35 from the *Progressive Farmer*. We mailed letters to editors of several weekly newspapers offering "exciting adventures by two journalists who plan to cycle through Europe. . . . Twenty stories, $2.50 each!" The response was hardly overwhelming, but five weeklies responded. Refunds from a Government SNAFU for overpaying our GI insurance were like pure gold.

The biggest problem was convincing our parents that bicycling was not a completely senseless thing to do. Hank's mother worried that we weren't putting money aside to buy a refrigerator. His grandmother was positive our ship would sink because the sea was no place for sane people. Indeed, it was difficult for my mother to comprehend at all, having been born in 1894, when tight corsets and ankle-length skirts were considered proper and it most difficult for women to ride newly-popular bicycles.

"But you told me women were liberated before the turn of the century and bloomers were introduced as the new cycling garb," I reminded her.

"Oh yes indeed. That's true," she agreed. "Even so, those baggy bloomers were like helium-filled knickerbockers and caused quite a sensation. Why, I remember the pastor of Waco's First Baptist Church considered it much too shocking and threatened to excommunicate any woman who dared come to church clad in that outrageous garment. I remember I was quite upset."

"That was then, mother. This is now. Things are different!"

"I've heard that before, too. Are you sure you want to do it?" she asked again. So when I mentioned that at the end of the summer we planned to use the educational provisions of the government's GI Bill to enroll for six weeks at a university in Switzerland, she became quite excited. We had registered for the only course they offered in English, appropriately titled: "Europe: Tradition and Change." Mother agreed we were halfway through the twentieth century and times were changing.

In the end, I think she would have joined us, but unfortunately she never learned to ride a bicycle. I considered mother "elderly" but at the time she was only fifty-six years of age.

Being a native Texan, used to Texan concepts of space and distance, mother found it difficult to understand the compactness of western Europe and the density of the population. Out of the back door of my folks' house in Brooks County, it was possible to look for eighty miles towards the Rio Grande without seeing more than good, open range country sparsely covered with mesquite and cactus. Over the sand dunes to the east was the Gulf of Mexico. She couldn't understand that where we planned to cycle, there would be tiny villages every few miles and likely historic castles or monuments at every corner.

I looked forward to attending the University in Fribourg, a mostly French-speaking city about thirty miles south of Bern. To be eligible for GI assistance we had to be able to at least read an elementary level French textbook. Hank said he learned all he needed to know from a small book issued to the "Soldiers of the Allied Forces of World War II."

My foreign language was limited to high school Spanish—"Mi casa es su casa"—and I was required to submit a Certificate of Eligibility, Government Form 11905-E. Thanks again to GI benefits, I was able to enroll in a conversational French course with the Linguaphone Institute and receive a package of 78-rpm records (in a case made of imitation leather), books and worksheets. Only after passing this course and receiving the certificate would I be able to submit an application for the six-week term.

Learning a new language wasn't easy for me, but I found French to be fascinating and full of grammatical gender. For instance, "knife" is masculine but "spoon" is feminine, and "brasserie" is not a woman's bra but an ale house. The final exam was to make a recording in French. Simple enough, despite an abundance of pesky "verbes irréguliers." The college music department was the only place in town with a microphone and electrical recording equipment. Actually, I sounded quite Frenchy: "Quels sont ces Bâteaux? A quelle distance suis-je de —? Je désire toucher un chèque" and "Et la danse en est une autre forme d'expression." Linguaphone officials sent a sharp response by return mail, something about sounding like it came from south of the Rio Grande.

The "two-for-one" passport.

The Veterans Administration notified Hank that he must establish his marital status to be eligible for an extra $30 for his "spouse" while at the University. Thirty dollars? Wow! By return mail, the clerk in Willacy County, Texas, sent a copy of our marriage certificate which we forwarded ASAP to the VA in Washington, D.C. So much for government red tape, especially since they did not respond to my note that I, too, was a veteran. Eventually two small green ID cards arrived from the American office of the university certifying that Henry L. Alsmeyer, Jr., and spouse—that's me— were officially registered. These cards would later be exchanged for permanent certificates.

The student health nurse gave us free tetanus and typhoid shots, but a certificate for smallpox vaccinations had to be signed by a physician. These shots cost a whopping $15. Our next concern was whether we should apply for individual passports at $10 each or pose together for the same price. We chose the latter, even though we looked as if we had stepped from Grant Wood's "American Gothic." It wasn't until later we realized that in addition to our passport, a luxuriant frontier jungle of other forms-in-triplicate, rubber stamped in red ink, awaited us.

I ordered three cotton blouses, advertised in *Seventeen* for $1.39 each, with my name embroidered on the Peter Pan collars. Most of my other clothes were left over from college days: a mustard color suit and a pair of uncomfortable platform shoes, a couple of wool skirts, white socks and loafers. Pants and shorts were frowned upon, Mary had written. I also took a bright red sweater that I had received as a Christmas gift years before. Carefully woven into it, white thread against red, was that familiar quotation: "O, wind, if winter comes, can spring be far behind?" Every time I wore it, I remembered how it once caught the eye of an English professor as he passed me on campus. He stopped and asked me who wrote it: Shelley or Keats? To this day, I still can't remember!

We took no raincoats and didn't own an umbrella. Hank packed a few pair of khakis, cotton shirts, his Sunday suit, an extra pair of size twelve shoes and his favorite garment, a GI field jacket. A $2.50 traveling iron was purchased at an appliance store that was going out of business. Our most expensive purchase was a camera, film, a light meter and related equipment. Our photographer friends, Forrest and Helen Shield, helped us select the best reflex camera we could afford, but failed to tell us how complicated it would be to adjust diaphragm and shutter speeds and something called optical eye-level views.

We booked passage on the *Oregon*, a French line freighter scheduled to sail from New Orleans after taking on cargo in Corpus Christi and Houston. Fortunately, Hank saw a tiny notice in the shipping news of the Corpus Christi *Caller-Times* that reported the *Oregon* was in port, and on a quiet Saturday afternoon in January we drove down to the pier to look it over. Along the way, I tried to explain a few nautical terms to Hank, but he said he had already crossed the Atlantic twice and all he needed was a bottle of pills for seasickness. The deep hollow sounds of brackish water swishing against the ship made me stop, for it brought back memories of many trips in navy ambulances to pick up wounded sailors and marines at Pier 9 in San Francisco. While on duty at Oak Knoll Naval Receiving Hospital, I had seen hundreds of "kids" ship out, only to return as hardened men, often on crutches and litters. I couldn't believe it had been only five or six years before.

On the *Oregon*, a few young Frenchmen in sharp uniforms came down the ramp, leaving a lone ensign standing on deck, the collar of his jacket turned up against the cutting winds that might eventually lead to a blue norther.

"May we come aboard?" I called, from the base of the gangplank. Hank moved to the shadow of a forklift as if he didn't know me at all! "We will sail on the *Oregon*. Soon! From New Orleans . . . in April!" The young ensign bowed and tipping his cap, motioned for us to come aboard.

"Come on, Hank. Let's go," I said, pulling him from behind the silent machinery. "I wonder if they still use bos'n whistles?"

"Don't ask me," he said, shrugging his shoulders. "I was no swabbie." The young officer motioned again and I was halfway up the ramp before Hank emptied his pipe.

"Welcome aboard. My name is Etienne. Steven in English," he said, introducing himself very formally. "As you can see, all my friends are on liberty while, unfortunately, I have duty. Come aboard, s'il vous plaît. You speak French? No? I learned to speak English in a few months by listening to passengers from America. I speak well?"

"Very well, indeed."

"You will learn French quickly," he said. "You are to sail on the *Oregon*? She's a fine little freighter. Let me give you a tour. Actually, she is a converted World War II American Liberty ship." He took us through the small dark lounge, then to the galley and dining area and finally down to the engine room. Large pieces of shiny machinery smelled of oil and fresh paint. It was awesomely silent, except for the sloshing sound of water outside.

I have always been fascinated by what goes on in the bowels of a ship. I remember when a couple of sailors in San Francisco proudly took my WAVE friend Mary Bryde and me down to the engine room of an LST, a barge-like ship used to transport tanks. Nothing can compare, however, to the time my friend from Scotland and I went exploring on the Delta Queen *in New Orleans many years later. We went down several flights of a newly-painted gray metal ladder, searching for the sounds of churning engines. We ended up inside a large room filled with glistening polished copper and brass machinery. The lonely machinist's mate was so surprised to see two middle-aged women in his hallowed grounds, he almost fainted!*

"Please. To my cabin, for a drink if you like," Etienne said, as we followed him down the passageway to officers' quarters. Hank was almost too tall to stand up straight in the small, neat cabin. Etienne pulled a chair from his desk for me. I noticed his bunk blanket had neatly squared corners, very GI.

"Benedictine?" he asked, as he went towards a cabinet. After carefully filling three small glasses, he held his high and said something in French. I took a sip. *Only* a sip, fortunately, for the potent liqueur swept like fire down to my toes; my lips wrinkled like a prune. Hank took a swallow and blinked. His face flushed and he broke out in sweat.

"AAHhhhh . . . Benedictine?" He coughed, wiping the Tabasco-like liquid from his lips. "MMMmmm. Well, it's different!"

Etienne laughed.

"I have been navigator for two years," he said. "I sign up as deck officer by-the-voyage, and after two or three crossings, I take time off and spend a month at the Riviera! When you sail from New Orleans in April, I will be waiting for you to come aboard." As we left, Hank promised to pick him up after lunch on Sunday when he was off duty.

By Sunday morning, the norther had blown over and it was again typical crisp January weather. We took Etienne to the Corpus Christi Naval Air Station, then across the causeway to Padre Island. The long sandy beach was deserted except for a few seagulls dipping and soaring over white-cap waves. What impressed him most were the vast fields waiting to be planted in spring cotton. In most fields we could see churning oil derricks, surrounded by tall blazing flares of natural gas. We had supper with Hank's parents—real southern fried chicken, Texas style, and thick cream gravy. Etienne told us his father was an engineer with the French embassy in Rome, his older brother—an engineer for an aircraft company—and his sister—a teacher of Greek, German and French at the high school level.

"Thank you for introducing me to Texas," Etienne said, as we took him back to the pier. "Whenever I see billowing clouds over the ocean or eat what you call southern fried chicken, I will think of y'all! You like my Texas accent? In New Orleans, I will be waiting."

How disappointed we were a few weeks later when the French line notified us that not only our schedule had been changed, but our freighter booking as well! We would now sail April 1 aboard the *Pont L'Evêque*.

We never saw the *Oregon* or Etienne again.

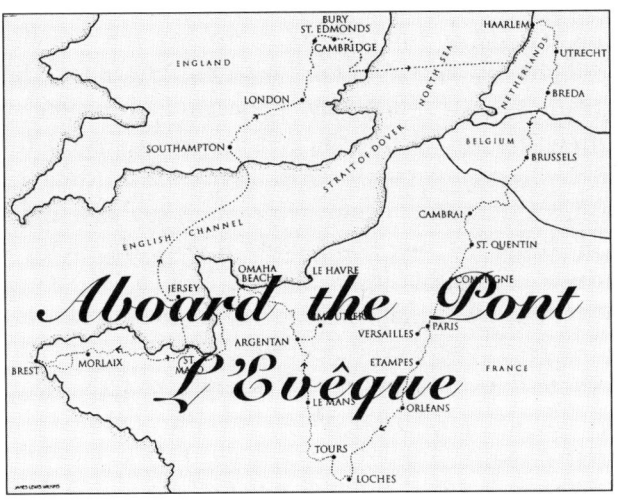

Aboard the Pont L'Évêque

The day of departure—my birth-day—finally arrived. Mother and dad had planned to drive us to New Orleans but that fell through when the water pump on the windmill went out. Hank's parents took us as far as a small hotel near the Southern Pacific railway station in Houston, and we caught the early train the next morning. As we waited restlessly in the terminal, I thought about the many changes in my life since I first sat on the same ornate wooden benches and stared at the same huge murals of Santa Anna surrendering at San Jacinto, when I was on my way to boot camp in 1943.

By early afternoon, through the train's windows, thick wooded marshes faded into the horizon and we could finally see the skyline of New Orleans. The train slowed, then crawled, across the long bridge spanning the Mississippi. New Orleans was everything I expected it to be, even the De Soto Hotel's "Low rates. Good service." Before dinner I phoned a friend of my father's who graciously invited us to meet him for brunch the next day at a very plush garden restaurant. Later, I called a friend I hadn't seen since navy days in San Francisco.

"What's up?" I asked.

"Changing diapers!" was the reply.

Ohhhh? Ooooo.

Being typical tourists, we walked through the French Quarter then boarded a big paddle wheeler for a tour down the Mississippi. It was quite exciting to see *our* little short-hulled freighter bobbing merrily up and down between huge cargo vessels and a few cruise ships, but I was disappointed we would not see our friend Etienne.

Near boarding time in late afternoon, we splurged and bought a bottle of cheap wine to celebrate our departure, not knowing we would be served large carafes of delicious French wine at every meal for the next three weeks! The moment I went aboard, I felt I was back in a civilization that was centuries old and at the same time highly modern even though the freighter was a relic of World War II. We were scheduled to sail at 7 A.M. on the first day of April. Most of the cabins were along a breezeway amidships, but fortunately, we were on the port side. A gentle breeze came in the open porthole of our cabin, which was larger than the others and had probably been used as officers' quarters during the war.

The cabin was sparsely fitted with a storage bench for our gear, a built-in desk, two straight chairs, a tiny closet and a small lavatory. Very narrow double-deck bunks were fitted with tight square-cornered sheets. The Head (toilet) was down the narrow passageway, and the shower someplace up a ladder.

Seven passengers sailed with us: a civil engineer, a newspaper reporter, an African agriculturist, two single fellows who were also planning a bicycle trip, and an older couple from Belgium. I was ready for a truly laid-back cruise, especially since everyone thought we were on our honeymoon! The Tillinghams, the distinguished-looking couple from Belgium, spoke fluent French even though their home was in San Francisco. They had spent the previous two weeks at the very expensive Shamrock Hotel in Houston, and paid an extra $150 so their dogs could travel with them. I felt sorry for poor Mrs. Tillingham, in a cabin half the size of ours with a 200-pound husband and three French poodles! If they had offered me that much cash, however, I might have changed cabins with them!

Captain L. LeRoux told us that the *Pont L'Evêque* was named for a small village in France that during the war had lost many homes and centuries-old buildings. The village is also known for its delicious cheese. Not the flamboyant Camembert or the creamy Neuchatel, but more the "hungry man's cheese." Hank, noting in his journal that the captain was from Morlaix, told him we would try to include it in our cycle tour.

A docking pilot directed the ship until it cleared the pier, then it was turned over to the harbor pilot. It took eight hours for the *Pont L'Evêque* to reach the Gulf of Mexico. The murky river was lined with small shacks balanced on wobbly stilts. Men waved from little dinghies that bobbed happily alongside. Huge white long-legged birds flitted about as an assortment of seagoing vessels followed a deep narrow path along mud islands and scrub brush. Captain LeRoux told us that river pilots were met by a pilot boat at the end of the river, and then another boat would take us out into the Gulf. At the tip of the river was a station where the pilot boarded a small plane and flew back to New Orleans. These pilots, he said, must be familiar with every channel, turn, and sandbar. Black buoys indicate the starboard side of the river; red buoys, port.

Eating dinner, especially the first few nights, was an experience in itself. As the ship swayed with the motions of the sea, my hand swept through the air as if I were directing an orchestra with my fork instead of a baton. Each menu was in a "Compagnie Générale Transatlantique" folder covered with a watercolor of Versailles, "Le Château au siècle de Louis XIV":

DÉJEUNER

Filets de hareng

Beurre

Salade de tomates

Rizotto Milannaise

Steacks grillés

Pommes Pont-Neuf

Fromage

Fruit

Café

***

DINER

Crème de cèleris

Petits pâtés Parisiens

Red Snapper poché
Poulet de grain roti
Pommes Cocettes
Salade
Fromages
Crêpes religieuses
Fruits
Thé

Large carafes of wine were served with every meal, and tea and pastries in the afternoon.

During one meal, we were served a gray-green vigorous plant the size of a hand grenade and shaped like a thorny cactus covered with prickly points. I looked at Hank. He shrugged his shoulders and wondered whether it was edible.

"I think it's called artichoke. Watch that lady from Belgium," I whispered. She carefully pulled off a pointed leaf and dipped it in buttery sauce. Slowly and deliberately, she sucked the tender part off. Delicious.

I stood on deck with the wind at my back, watching a group of seamen all dressed in denim jackets and baggy pants. One dark sailor, probably from the south of France or North Africa, looked up, and in a deep throaty voice said, "My name is Cassin." Pulling his black leather beret down on his dark curly hair, he continued to unwind a pile of ropes near the gunwale. I honestly believe if he had said, "Call me Ishmael," I would swear he had stepped from the pages of Herman Melville's book of a hundred years before. He pointed to the unusually smooth ocean and said, "Called 'cat's paw'. Storm coming."

It was Cassin who came to our cabin a few days later when my little travel iron blew a fuse. In only a few minutes, he changed the wiring and, with a sympathetic look at Hank, shrugged his shoulders and patiently pointed out the difference between AC and DC currents.

On the third day, Captain LeRoux invited us below to the galley. The crew's cat had just had five new kittens, their eyes still not open. The cook took a loaf of warm bread from the oven and, cutting a slice, spread it thick with butter and handed it to me. I ate it savagely.

As we neared Key West, the sea around us suddenly exploded with bottle-nosed dolphins gracefully leaping and twisting in and out of the water, showering us with spray. They swam so close we could see the dark rings around their eyes and notice that one had a patch on his back like a saddle. For twenty minutes, they wove their magic around us. Then just as suddenly as they had come, they vanished.

From high above the deck on the navigation bridge, I stood in the cold biting wind, fascinated by the lazy white-topped ripples that stretched as far as my eyes could see. Captain LeRoux and Hank stood inside the wheelhouse and, as expected, talked about the weather.

"I am amazed at the similarity in weather reporting," Hank said. "Right after the war when I was stationed at Orly Field outside Paris, we received weather reports day and night by radio teletypewriter. It was fascinating. They came from almost every continent and we relayed them on to the Pentagon."

"Aboard the *Pont L'Evêque*, we take weather readings every six hours and send them to the Weather Bureau in Washington," Captain LeRoux said. "Later on, as we get farther into the Atlantic, our reports will be sent to France. Of course, during hurricane season or times of severe weather conditions, our readings are taken and reported every thirty minutes." A bell rang and the captain nodded slightly and excused himself.

"I can never understand why men are so fascinated by weather," I said as Hank and I climbed slowly down the ladder.

"It's because weather is so unpredictable . . . like women," he teased.

In 1992, I wrote the agent of a freight line company to ask if they had information about the Pont L'Evêque *or any converted World War II Liberty ships that sailed forty or more years ago. The agent responded with a note saying, "I'm sorry, but we cannot help you with details about carrying passengers in 1950. Actually, I wasn't even born then."*

At Sea

*S*omeone once said an ocean is free to all nations, subject to none. It is awesome to think all this salt water covers three-fourths of the earth yet generates so much wasted energy! Waves moving in rough white swells, back and forth; entrancing, tranquilizing like other rhythms of nature. Day after day. Year after year. Century after century. It all seems so effortless, one wave following another choreographed by God. The gently moving blue-gray ridges swell to the surface as far as eyes can see, leaving sharp outlines of foaming curves. We have been at sea a week and still no "mal de mer." Each day eases into the next, seemingly blending together until it is hard to believe that time is passing so quickly.

Mild ocean swells turned dark gray, and a reflection of the somber cloud cover descends from a low pressure area. Suddenly we found ourselves in the center of violent torrents of wind and rain off of the Carolinas. The weather cleared a little, only to form into another deep trough charging down from Newfoundland. The ship's bow rose high and then slapped down with a shudder, and the *Pont L'Evêque* turned off course to prevent more battering.

Hank and I pushed open the lounge door and, bracing against hurricane-like winds as we held to the guard rail, inched our way forward on the slippery deck. What a sensation—like riding a gigantic roller coaster that lifted perhaps twenty-feet from the stormy sea— then fell with a huge splash back into the ocean. The sky became even more threatening and azure blues surrendered to angry clouds of blackness. No longer was the sea an expanse of liquid sapphire sparkling in the sun, but more a manipulative gray monster, violently tossing us about with angry waving arms. Seamen in yellow trench coats and knee-high boots ordered us inside and hurriedly roped off the area. Hank retired to our cabin a bit nauseated, but I joined the other passengers who had rattled about in the lounge like marbles in a teacup. Dining room chairs were anchored down and brackets bolted to tables to hold plates and glasses.

Every loose item in our cabin had been tossed about as if hit by a tornado. During the night, the ship continued to surge through rough seas. I climbed to the top bunk, but not for long. Between threats of nausea, I laid there, humming the beautiful Navy hymn, "Eternal Father, Strong to Save." When I was at WAVES boot camp, I remember laughing as we sang the second line about sailors asking to be protected "from these RESTLESS WAVES." It wasn't so humorous now. Seamen through the ages have sailed through this "chaos dark and rude—to the angry tumult deep."

There was no way I could stay in that top bunk! About midnight I sought the comfort of Hank's warm body as I crawled into his narrow bunk below. As I pressed tightly against the bulkhead and the ship reeled to and fro like a drunken seaman, I finally dozed off to sleep with the hymn's final words loud and clear: "Oh hear us when we cry to thee, for those in peril on the sea." I was not surprised when Captain LeRoux announced the next morning that he had changed our estimated time of arrival. This would make a seven- or eight-day delay in reaching Le Havre.

The converted Liberty ship was definitely made exclusively for an all-male crew, especially in the closet-sized Head down the narrow passage. About midnight during the stormiest of storms, I felt my way along the dimly lit passage without too much difficulty. As expected, on a ship built during the war for all-male sea crews, the toilet seat had been "programmed" to stay up. I can go along with that. Holding on to the door frame, I pushed the wooden seat down. Before I could turn around and sit on it, the sudden motion of the ship made it spring up and I would find myself thrown forward, grasping the water pipe on the opposite wall. Try again. This went on for several minutes until finally during a sudden calm, I succeeded. So much for sea duty. . . .

Time seemed to stand still during several more days of rough storms, then the sea suddenly calmed and a hazy sun crept up over new gentle waves. I was getting anxious even though it would still be several days before we steamed into the English Channel.

"Unfortunately, we have missed the tide, which is sometimes over twenty-feet high. That is why two locks are needed in this harbor. I am afraid you will not arrive in Paris until about mid-afternoon tomorrow," Captain LeRoux apologized. As the port of Le Havre appeared far on the eastern horizon, he said we must now wait for the *Pont L'Evêque* to pick up the pilot boat at noon. Hank was anxious to notify Mary about our time of arrival at the Paris train terminal and Captain LeRoux graciously worded a cablegram, saving us a few francs which we didn't have in the first place.

The port was a busy place. After the war, France was in a pitiful state of destruction. Here in Le Havre, people seem still angry over the severe bombing raids by Allied air forces which were done to prevent the Nazis' use of the port.

"I remember my first impression of Le Havre," Hank said, leaning against the rail and wiping salty spray from his face. "It was awfully cold. Not far from the ship were remains of submarine shelters with eight-foot thick walls. Some had been destroyed during air attacks. After we struggled down the gangplank with our duffel bags and other gear, we had to wait on a pile of rubble that was used as a temporary pier. A group of German prisoners of war was working nearby and one yelled: 'Anyone there from Texas?' I answered 'here.' Then the fellow asked if I knew his cousin Joanna Schmidt from a little German settlement in the center of Texas. The POW seemed such an ordinary sort of guy, I hated to disappoint him.

"We boarded a troop train of rattling third class cars, and settled down for the night. I had never been so cold! The cars must have been strafed or bombed. Most of the windows were gone, and there were other signs of destruction. We were issued C-rations before going to sleep.

"It was even worse the next few days in ice cold tents at a 'repple depple,' a replacement depot outside Chateau-Thierry. We ate our Thanksgiving turkey from mess kits. It was astonishingly good though. I even had time to walk to town to see where father's 'Blue Ridge' Division had been stationed during the World War I Chateau-Thierry Campaign. Then we boarded trucks for the long cold ride to Paris. Fortunately, I rode in the cab with the driver. We were quartered in a large department store that had been converted to barracks, and, finally another truck took us out to Orly Field." His eyes seemed glued to the horizon as if he were hunting for something.

"Hank, it's getting too cold out here," I said, after a long silence. "Let's go in." I turned and went back to our warm cabin, but Hank remained on deck, apparently lost in his thoughts.

Le Havre, one of France's most important ports, was seen by many servicemen during the war. Often called the "Main Street of the Seine," it has been a seaport since the seventeenth century, though now expanded greatly by dredging out large channels and turning basins. To the north, we noticed tall cliffs lined with a few very modern and expensive homes, but the older homes below had that tired look of survival. Most construction seemed to be at the port since the Seine served as the highway for the endless flow of barges that transported much of the commerce to and from Europe.

With the arrival of the German troops in 1940, the die was cast for the port's eventual destruction. German submarines began scavenging the Atlantic in an effort to starve out Great Britain and block American aid. But bombing raids by Allied forces continued and eventually only twenty percent of the city's buildings were left standing.

"Following the war, work on the docks has taken precedence over new housing," Captain LeRoux told us. "Without the docks, Le Havre would be a town without a purpose—and I would be without a ship. We cannot control the sea, however. I am sorry the weather has again delayed our arrival, and it will be morning before the tide changes."

"After three weeks at sea, what's twelve more hours?" Hank replied, as waves gently swayed the ship to and fro. We spent the rest of the morning watching workers across the way pour cement for new pier foundations, making Le Havre a great naval and commercial port again. My eyes had little time for anything but the fascinating spectacle of ships and wharves. Early the next morning we stood on deck, watching crane operators as they swung cargo aboard ships with effortless precision, tons at a time. The harbor pilot seemed unconcerned as he swung our little ship through an opening with only inches to spare. Another crewman gauged with only a slight glance, the exact spot to drop a thick pad to keep the ship's side from scraping the quay.

"Le Havre today has only one thing in common with my first landing," Hank said. "In 1945, it was hurry up and wait. This is a far cry from debarking as private, US Army Air Force, serial number 18233829. As different as night and day! For someone brought up in Texas, I had to pinch myself when I found I was to be sent to Paris. In those days, people didn't travel to Europe very much. I never thought that I would actually be here. Every weekend, every pass, I went somewhere, regardless of how little money I had.

"Travel cost next to nothing and people were unusually kind to servicemen, especially if we could give them a package of American cigarettes. There were several tricks and secrets for GIs all over the Continent. I was determined that I would do it again—and here we are. Am I excited? You bet!"

We were up early waiting for the ship to enter port. Custom officials came aboard to check our passport and before long, we went ashore and boarded the French line shuttle—a glorified taxi—for the auto rail terminal. Captain LeRoux assured us that if we reach the terminal by noon there would be plenty of time for the eighty-mile-an-hour auto rail to Paris. A representative of the Bank of France usually came aboard to change travelers checks into francs, but had not been to our ship because of its unscheduled arrival. I felt as if I were floating as I made my way through the damaged terminal that still seemed not quite ready for foreign travelers. There was no booth to exchange foreign currency, so Hank hurried to the nearest hotel to change one of our precious American Express checks into French francs. I waited for him near our luggage, and was surprised that he came running back a few minutes later.

"I need our passport—on the double!" he called above the bustling noise. I kept our passport safely in my black leather GI purse that hung from my shoulder. It still had my maiden name embossed in gold letters inside. Off he went again. We had only about fifteen minutes to purchase tickets, retrieve our luggage from the station cart, and board the train for Paris.

All this rushing, and we *still* missed the fast auto rail! An ancient steam locomotive was scheduled to leave at 7 P.M., but it was too late to notify Mary. Besides, buying two one-way tickets left us with only a handful of small coins and Hank remembered how difficult French telephones were to operate. It was obvious the third-class car we eventually boarded had been through trying days. There was no heat. Freezing cold rain began to fall, but I wasn't worried. We had arrived! Words couldn't describe my excitement, as I picked up our portable typewriter and hurried towards the first open compartment door I saw. Hank followed close behind, pushing a three-wheel cart with the rest of our gear.

"Yes, this is a far cry from debarking in '45 as a GI from Texas," Hank said again, as we settled down for the slow journey in the dead of night. The engine gave one last whistle, then a hissing belch of steam, and slowly moved forward with stuttering groans. An elderly man in a faded black suit and round black hat opened the compartment door and quietly sat across from us. He pushed a small wicker basket under his seat, gave a deep sigh and closed his eyes. Gently, so not to wake the old gentleman, Hank untangled his long legs, and moved to the narrow passageway just outside the compartment door. Rolling hills were dimly visible on this cold rainy night, and scattered lights blinked from small villages across the horizon. Hank smoked his pipe as if hypnotized by the click-clack of metal wheels over rough worn rails. His eyes seemed to be searching for something. I wondered: is he remembering the little Canadian WAC he met at Versailles? Orly Field? His Air Corps buddies? Or is he just anxious to see the Grillets again?

The old man shuffled his feet, leaned over with great effort, then took his basket from under the wooden seat. He opened it slowly and carefully unfolded a large white napkin. I watched every movement. He unwrapped heavy butcher paper from thick slices of bread, a hunk of dark strong cheese, and a generous piece of ham. O-o-o-o, it smelled so good! Finally, he pulled out a bottle of dark cloudy homemade wine, took a sip then slowly wiped his purple-stained lips with the back of his hand. As an afterthought, he pulled a small knife from his pocket, cleaned it on his pants, and cut a huge slice from a juicy red apple. I could almost taste it!

I was tired and remembered we hadn't had anything to eat since our early morning breakfast aboard the *Pont L'Evêque*. I watched enviously as the old man put his basket under the hard bench again, then leaned back and began to snooze softly. He looked as comfortable as a baby in a crib. But the wooden seats were much too hard for me. I couldn't get comfortable. Finally lights from small villages became more plentiful. Could we actually be arriving in Paris, I wondered. Were we *really* to visit the Louvre and the Eiffel Tower? I still couldn't believe it.

Everything was quiet except for the rattle of train wheels on the narrow rail and an occasional far-off whistle. The rain changed to a soft drizzle, and thunder rumbled in the distance. I looked at Hank standing just outside the door in the train's narrow passage, smoke from his pipe making slow circles towards the cracked window. He was unaware of the passengers who squeezed past him. There was no doubt in my mind, he was once again Private Henry Louis Alsmeyer, Jr., 18233829, AAF 762d BU—132d ACS Sqn. Det 225 APO 886 New York. Remembering. . . .

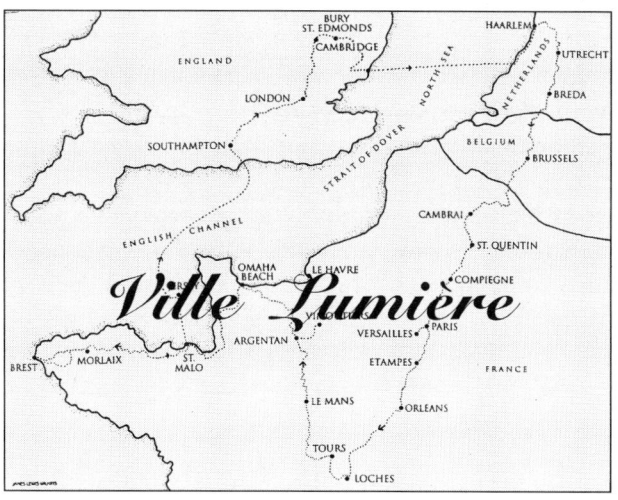

$\mathscr{P}$aris—Ville Lumière—The City of Light. The brilliant glow was visible in the sky for miles around. I was quite anxious, especially because I was desperately hungry. Near midnight our train crawled into the terminal, gave one last belch of steam, and groaned to a stop. The "lumière" of Paris was nothing compared to the brilliant glow on Hank's face when he saw the Grillets waving to him from the platform below. We hadn't expected anyone to meet us at this late hour, but there they were: Mary and her two daughters, Anne Marie and Claude.

"I can't get over how much the girls have grown," Hank said after I was introduced to everyone. He wrapped his arms around Anne Marie and Claude. "And I guess Jean is almost as tall as I am!"

"Oh yes. He's almost sixteen now," Mary said proudly. "M. Grillet sends his regards." We chatted a few minutes then rescued our luggage from a nearby cart.

"I have just the place for you," Mary said, as we all crowded into a boxy little taxi. "Hotel du Palais. Small, but I think you will like it. It is quite inexpensive and located in the old part of the city near the

Ile de la Cité." The cab stopped near a dim streetlight in front of a tiny hotel squeezed between a small restaurant and a flower shop.

"These are my friends from America," Mary said as an elderly woman unlocked the door with a huge key. "From TEXAS," she emphasized, for the little woman appeared to be a bit deaf.

Turning to us, she said, "I know you are tired. We'll leave you now. We look forward to your visit to Draveil after you've had a wonderful week or two here in Paris."

We stood on the worn stone step of the small hotel and watched Mary's taxi speed away, then turned again to the old woman.

"Ah. TEX-a-a-sss!" she mumbled as she wiped her hands on her apron and led us up narrow squeaking stairs. It was dark as pitch until she flicked a time-regulated light switch. A dim single bulb suddenly flashed on, then turned off almost before we reached the other end of the hall. She took an oversized key from a ring and handed it to Hank.

The ceiling was higher than the width of the room, and taking up most of the floor space was a beautiful antique bed covered with an inviting down comforter. A tall fireplace stretching to the ceiling was haloed by a gold frame mirror. Our typewriter and few pieces of luggage were lost in the highboy. The room had a wonderfully strange mixture of colors: a worn green velvet chair, very old deep-red carpet, marbleized bedside table, and a lamp with a hideous gold shade casting shadows on ornate but faded wallpaper. A lavatory and a strange little thing called a bidet were tucked away in the far corner. The WC (water closet) was across the hall with a few newspapers to read or use as necessary. No toilet paper. A small sign hanging from the ceiling read "Tirer la chasse," meaning "pull the toilet chain." A bath would cost five francs, about two cents, if we could endure the icy cold water. All for 350 francs, or $1.40 a night!

Heavy faded drapes framed large French doors that opened to a small balcony overlooking Pont-Neuf, the oldest bridge on the Seine. To the left was the Ile de la Cité. Streetlights outlined the sturdy twin towers of Notre Dame Cathedral standing solidly where an altar to a river god once stood. Across the river opposite our hotel we saw the uppermost parts of Sainte-Chapelle, the royal chapel dating to the thirteenth century, famous for its stained glass windows.

A cathedral clock struck the hour of midnight. I reminded Hank that we hadn't eaten since breakfast. Rubbing my aching feet

Notre Dame Cathedral, near the Alsmeyers' hotel.

didn't seem to ease the hunger pains. Surely it's not too late to cash another traveler's check and find a place to eat? Earlier, Mary had offered to loan us a few francs until we could get to a bank the next day, but in all of our excitement, she forgot. We were almost flat broke. Tiptoeing down the dark hallway, Hank pressed the light switch and we crept down the squeaky stairs, the old lady watching our every move.

It was dark and cold as we walked a couple of blocks to the Hôtel De Ville, the famous City Hall of Paris. We crossed the street towards the theater featuring the American movie, "Annie du Far West." At each small pub or cafe, cashiers looked at our American

Express checks and shook their heads and said no. Our only alternative was to take the Metro that laced like a spider web under the streets. During the next week or so, we found it to be truly "l'indispensable" just as Mary had said. Hank put the last few coins in the meter and we were soon on our way to the Avenue des Champs Elysées. The main boulevard was totally different from the Chatelet metro stop area where we were staying. In a plush hotel, the night clerk looked at our wrinkled clothes, but cashed our checks without question. It was well past midnight before we finally ate at the smoky hotel bar.

The next morning, a light tap on the door woke me to a sunfilled room. I slipped from the warm comforter and tiptoed to the door. The little old lady was smiling broadly. "Café au lait?" she asked, as she handed me a tray with a pot of bitter coffee, a tiny pitcher of milk, and two large croissants fresh from the baker. For eighty francs—twenty-five cents—we had breakfast in bed almost every morning.

It is difficult after forty-five years to remember everything about our first visit to Paris. Of course, I still have copies of the feature stories Hank sent to weekly newspapers in South Texas, and my letters home were filled with great anticipation of things to come. I remember it was one glorious adventure after another, and especially that we arrived on the 21st day of April, 1950, after three long weeks at sea.

We were every bit the ordinary American students, spending the first few days strolling across sixteenth-century bridges to the Left Bank, stopping at bookstalls along the Seine. Hank read every brass historical marker on dull gray buildings as we prowled the narrow tree-lined streets. I preferred listening to Paris pigeons, for they seemed to coo differently than the ones at home. And I wanted to stop at every pâtisserie and eat flaky, gooey, sweet pastries that made me sticky-faced like a kid when I licked my fingers. Except for the withered old women slowly sweeping the streets with homemade brooms, traffic looked remarkably like that in Dallas. Cars roared down the wide streets quickly and furiously, tootling instead of honking. Most amazing of the automobiles were the dangerous little two-seat cars that looked like glorified motor scooters.

The ballet technique used by the gendarme directing traffic in the middle of the street is difficult to describe. He fluttered both

Scene from the Left Bank section of Paris.

hands high in the air, then rocked back on one foot and then the other, swinging his arm from side to side. He twirled and bowed, facing one way directing traffic and holding his other hand behind his back as if counting down the seconds with his fingers. In the midst of all this, with a thousand little waves and smiles and the dramatic flourish of a great conductor, he kept traffic flowing smoothly.

Pierre Ravias, agent in the A. Parrish Showroom just off of the Avenue des Champs Elysées, came to the door of his agency to ask

A spring morning among the book stalls on the Left Bank.

A helpful gendarme with Marie Alsmeyer, on a
Paris street.

if we could possibly be two of the buyers whose names had been placed on a year-long waiting list. After explaining we were only students from America admiring the Simcas, Renaults and Citroens, he proceeded to tell us how difficult it was to own an automobile in France. In the furious race for currencies, especially American dollars, French Fords are frequently exported to Spain, Denmark or the Netherlands.

"French people cannot buy foreign-made automobiles," he said. "They are sold only to Americans living here." American cars were known to be heavier and easier to handle, more powerful and quieter, but French automobiles used less fuel, which was selling for a steep fifty-three cents a gallon. Pierre said about 300 Renaults were made daily in France during 1949, compared with more than five million automobiles turned out in Detroit.

I listened politely but was more interested in the aroma of freshly-baked pastries that came from the shop next door. That's how we met George Couteau, proprietor of a tiny pâtisserie. He brought our tea and pastries then pulled a chair to our table for a chat. "Not from England, I see," he said as an introduction. "I know because you do not ask for cream in your tea! My name is George. I learned to speak English in North Africa with the French Air Force."

He and Hank carried on a French-English conversation, Hank telling him he had been stationed at Orly Field after the war, and the baker listing the great historic places we should visit in the beautiful city. Then George said, "I have a request to make of you, my American friends. Is it possible for you to send me a football helmet like I see your players wear in the movies? I ride a motorcycle, as do most Parisians, and French helmets are too bulky and heavy. If possible, I would like royal green and gold like the Irish of Notre Dame," he added. "I cannot pay you in American money, but you would be fully reimbursed." My mind went immediately to a tray of sticky pastries.

George went on to tell how he helped save the lives of eight Americans during the war, not in France or French North Africa, but instead halfway around the globe! He had been transferred to French Indochina after the liberation of North Africa. The French colony just south of China was still occupied by Japan, but caution and the complexities of international law allowed the French to transfer troops to the colony. Discharged from active duty, in due time George became manager of a hotel in Tonkin, the Hôtel du Coq d'Or—the Golden Rooster.

Soon afterward, American airmen began aerial sweeps along the mainland, and from one of these raids came George's chance to help. Shot down just off the southern coast of French Indochina, some Americans were rescued in a small French boat. Evading the Japanese, the boat reached shore, where the Americans were turned over to French soldiers then immediately loaded into fast trucks to cross the country during the night.

Still bitter against the Japanese, George recalled that he had kept the Americans hidden at his hotel in Tonkin for several days until they could be transferred to a French hospital. The Americans later made it safely north to China through the Underground.

"Several Americans returned to my hotel after the area was liberated. We had big parties. V-e-r-r-r-y big parties. Plenty of champagne. And beer. I especially remember two fellows named George

O'Ryan and Hugh Pope. Unfortunately, I no longer have their addresses. If you ever have a chance to meet them, say George—from the Hôtel du Coq d'Or in Tonkin—would like to hear from them."

"I'll do that," Hank said, making a note in his journal of George's friends. "But wouldn't you rather have a maroon and white football helmet instead of gold?" he asked, giving a Texas Aggie thumbs-up sign.

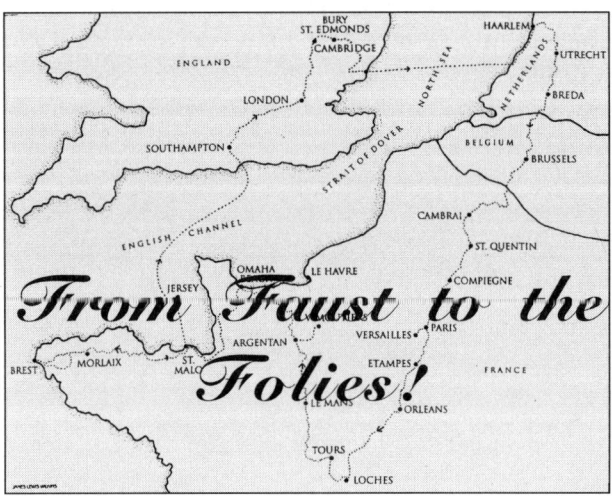

From Faust to the Folies!

$\mathcal{N}$ot to be outdone by wealthier Americans visiting Paris, we purchased tickets to the Théâtre National de L'Opéra. On our budget, it was a toss-up between *Faust* or *Figaro*. Each ticket would cost $1.75. *Faust* won, and we went on "Lundi, 24 avril."

The opera house, built in about 1875, is still considered one of the most splendid palaces ever erected for music, acting and dancing. The prosperity of France under the reign of Napoleon III is evident in the profusion of art of that period on display. Wide marble stairs led up to the second level where a lovely young woman handed us a program. She pulled aside red velvet drapes to reveal a magnificent view of gleaming gold and crimson colors below our box seats. Men in tuxedos and black ties escorted women wearing diamond rings and long dresses. Star-spangled jewelry glittered and caught the light, sending shades of it shimmering back to us.

After our taste of high culture, we decided a trip to Paris would not be complete without going to the *Folies Bergères*. At least that's what Hank said. The *Folies* bubbled for more than three hours with music, singing, comedy, and lots of "etc." High kicking cancan girls exploited the thrill of skirts raised to reveal flashing legs. This was followed by women in frilly costumes and a variety of acts from "Snow White and the Seven Dwarfs" to a mock wedding and a parade of Scottish dancers in kilts. The house suddenly exploded with laughter during the finale when the "Peter Sisters," a trio of very fat black women, floated down to the stage. On parachutes!

Paris is a lovely, mysterious place, crowded with the unexpected. I still remember the thrill I got when I saw the unutterably funny gargoyles hanging precariously along the top of Notre Dame Cathedral. I tried to imagine how many years it had taken the stonemasons to carve the wild and fantastic fire-breathing monsters from Greek mythology. Even when the cathedral didn't need more gargoyles to drain water from the roof, stonemasons continued to carve the imaginary monsters they called "chimaeras."

At an entrance to the Metro, Hank studied the map of Paris's long streets crossing from west to east and north to south, meeting

Gargoyles from the Notre Dame Cathedral.

at the Seine near the Ile de la Cité. Every distance from Paris to the borders of France is measured from this point. One could start walking towards Notre Dame on the roads of Normandy or Provence and find they all center inwardly to the Cathedral. Narrow streets would dwindle away, then suddenly open onto squares teaming with people. In Roman times, this area was only a small fishing village. It didn't take long for me to imagine myself a true Parisian atop a Gallic blockhouse near the part of the Seine that makes a great bow before meandering off toward Le Havre.

On Wednesday, it took us only ten minutes to walk to the Louvre, a dusty maze of dark galleries crammed with paintings hung floor to ceiling. Sweeping staircases, vaulted ceilings, high cathedral windows, marble floors and sculptured facades were constant reminders of the Louvre's colorful history that began in 1200 when King Philippe Auguste feared invasion by his Norman enemies. But it was the art from Napoleon's far-flung conquests that made the Louvre so fascinating. The famous *Mona Lisa*, much smaller than I expected, had eyes that seemed to follow me as I slowly backed away from the tiny roped-off area.

Across the square was the church of St. Etienne du Mont, and farther away, the enormous Pantheon, once a church but now a national monument where the remains of Hugo, Voltaire, Rousseau and several other notables are buried. The tomb of the eighteenth-century explorer and navigator Louis Antoine de Bougainville was especially meaningful.

I am amazed that the name Bougainville takes us around the world from Paris to South Texas, to the San Francisco Bay area and on to the Solomon Islands in the southwestern Pacific. Growing up in South Texas, we were quite familiar with the brilliant purple floral bracts of the tropical shrub named for this famous explorer. The name Bougainville also brought to mind my duties as a Navy corpsman, when I went in ambulances to meet hospital ships with casualties from the Pacific island of that name.

No one should visit Paris without touching one of Rodin's famous sculptures. Early Friday morning we found the life-size muscular figure *The Thinker* almost hidden in a small garden area. I read about the original wax cast of this particular sculpture being in a Kentucky museum, and how Rodin's realistic sculptures caused a furor when critics claimed he must have cast from a living person to achieve such perfection. Rodin proved the accusation false by producing the model who had posed for him.

I can't remember now whether it was the high winds or Hank's inability to smoke his pipe there that prevented us from venturing more than halfway up the 984-foot-tall Eiffel Tower. Hank reminisced about the time he viewed the magnificent structure from a low-level flight in the cockpit of an Army Air force C-47, or civilian DC-3. He says that spring evening flight gave him enough memories to last a lifetime. We were glad to see that the symbol of Paris was fully repaired from the effects of the war, even though no one yet has figured out what the tower is good for! Even Parisians admit it is ugly, but still everyone loves it.

I did get to the top of it some years later when my daughter Ann and I took the elevator and had an unforgettable view of the city. Even then, Hank stayed on the ground, smoking his pipe.

We strolled along quiet, curiously-named little streets that seemed to disappear into small city squares. We got lost several times, even though Hank tried to read the street signs then trace hypothetical routes on his map. I never knew which direction we were going, but followed him closely, for I was confident we would eventually end up in another fascinating place. Hank spoke French fairly well, but I didn't say more than "bonjour" and "merci." An elderly woman at a flea market assumed I was deaf because I stood expressionless in front of her cart as she rattled along about her wares. She looked at Hank and shook her head as she pointed to her ear. Finally, she saw my name embroidered on the collar of my blouse, and leaning over towards Hank, whispered softly, "Ah, petit Marieee!"

We got a late start on Saturday morning, and had lunch at the YMCA on the second floor of an old building on a dark side street. It was just like being in school again when, cafeteria style, we joined a long line of students and young people speaking many languages: English, Italian, French, and German dialects. The meal was good and inexpensive but I preferred the sidewalk chatter of the native Parisians. It's funny about French. No matter what the subject is, the language sounds like poetry to me, as if everyone is cooing words of love to each other. However, behind all the rich vowels and rolling R's, they're probably saying "My feet hurt."

After lunch, we joined shoppers who carried colored satchels and picked around in stacks of shoes, clothing and kitchen utensils displayed in front of large department stores. Male clerks in long black jackets stood alongside tables filled with an assortment of goods. One rather heavy woman held a very large stay-studded corset close to her body, checking for size; a man sat on the curb, trying on a new pair of shoes. Inside the Galeries Lafayette and Aux Louvre were small glass-enclosed elevators and newly-installed escalators much like those in Joske's in San Antonio. Clerks speaking chipped British-English at information booths were selling nylons for 750 to 900 francs a pair, along with American-made soaps like Lux and Palmolive, and Colgate toothpaste—all priced too high for the ordinary French working person. And for us as well.

Sidewalk clerks selling their goods "aux Galeries Lafayette."

Sidewalk shopping in Paris.

A small riot soon created a traffic jam on the sidewalk in front of a wide show window. We joined the noisy group of men and women who crowded together, clapping and whistling as beautiful models presented a free poor man's style show. Inexpensive dresses designed much like Dior originals were available on the sixth floor, a salesman announced above ear-splitting background music.

Strolling by sidewalk restaurants, reading the handwritten menus placed outside the windows, was always delightfully relaxing. After walking all day, I was anxious to have dinner at the family-style restaurant, La Poissarde, near our hotel. We arrived at 6 P.M., a proper time for supper in Texas, but were told it would be at least two hours before the cook gave a thought to preparing the evening meal. Our mistake was a great joke to the waitresses, but it wasn't long before we learned their schedule and were considered regular customers. Meals cost less than a dollar and were great combinations of pork roast or chops, potatoes (always pommes!) and a green salad. Delicious bread, of course, and white wine instead of water.

We were surprised when the cook came to our table and said he was curious about his new customers. In limited French, I tried to explain that we hoped to bicycle around Normandy and Brittany. Then on a piece of paper, I printed "America" and "Texas" and drew a tiny ship and two bicycles and wrote "France" and "England" and "Holland." He shook Hank's hand excitedly and told a waitress to bring us a bottle of house wine. Looking at my red sweater, he asked what was written on it. An obliging customer came to my rescue and told him it was a poem by the famous English poet, Shelley, and then interpreted it without error.

Paris doesn't actually wake up until about noon, much to Hank's delight, because he doesn't either. In fact, Parisians say evening lasts twelve hours—from five to five. At dusk, we stopped at pleasant sidewalk cafés and watched policemen in luminous white capes direct early evening traffic. On this Sunday evening, we joined strollers in Montmartre for pommes frites, at cafés with strange names like Fishmonger, Pig's Foot, Contented Father, and most unusual, a tiny place called the Dog That Smokes. The Crab was on a narrow winding street around the corner from our hotel and its proprietor was delighted to visit with Americans, especially a sergeant from Texas who had been at Orly.

"This part of the city has always been the center of Paris, beginning with the earliest conquerors. Through the years, one century has mingled with another, and life goes on," he said, wiping his hands on his apron.

"Perhaps too few servicemen realize this sense of continuity, but those of us who did grew to love the city," Hank replied. "We plan to go to the famous farmer's market soon."

"Ah, Les Halles, only a short distance from here. We call it the 'Stomach of Paris.' I buy my produce there. For more than seven centuries, Les Halles has stood in the same place. Even the most recent buildings were built hundreds of years ago. It will never grow old. Several small restaurants at the market are famous for onion soup. Go an hour or so after midnight."

We went back to the hotel, and I fell across the bed, exhausted. Hank studied his maps in the dim lamp light until early morning, then woke me for the short walk to the market sheds before Paris rumbled into a new dawn. Great piles of fresh produce as beautiful as a Renaissance painting glistened in the reflection of overhead lights: vine-ripened tomatoes, golden squash, eggplant and bell peppers—red, green, and yellow—and all sorts of strange fruits.

Small shops with flower seeds, potted plants, fishing and hunting supplies surrounded the small workingman's café where we found the famous onion soup. When the large bowl was placed in front of me I tried to separate long threads of cheese—Parmesan, Gruyere, or whatever—from chunks of bread that floated to the top. A few men in denim overalls began to laugh, and I knew I was not the first American they had seen covered with strings of cheese. Finally, one man slapped the table to get my attention, raised his spoon high, then slowly and deliberately began wrapping long threads of cheese around his spoon like spaghetti. After that, I found it quite simple. He tipped his cap and smiled broadly.

As we left Les Halles, the early morning sun was beginning to rise over ancient roofs and smoke was swirling from tall chimney pots. Fresh dew began to lift from the lovely gray city and as we walked slowly over a bridge, I thought of one of my favorite hymns, "Morning has broken, for a new day. . . . Sweet the rains new fall, sunlit from heaven."

I felt that George Gershwin must have written "American in Paris" especially for me on that first day of May. The temperature had dropped during the night and clouds covered the sky, and the short glimpses of sun appeared between frequent showers followed by bitter cold winds, but the trees along the Seine had turned green with new leaves and perfumed flowers filled the marketplace.

I have heard that during the month of May, peasants in Germany plant trees in front of their cowsheds, one for each cow and horse. In Ireland, they fasten green boughs against their huts to ensure plenty of milk. The Scots tie bows to cows' tails. But the most beautiful celebration is here in Paris, where from dawn to dusk flower vendors are calling "Fleurissez-vous mesdames. Achetez du bonheur. Voilà du joli muguet"—Wear a lily for luck, lady. Each vendor carries a basket or pushes his cart filled with nosegays and sprigs of Lily of the Valley. In rural areas it was truly a farmer's festival—a day of praying for rain and good crops and to frighten the witches away.

But in Paris on May 1, 1950, for this young couple, it was a festival of love. Hank hurried to buy lace-wrapped sprigs of lily before we had our mid-morning coffee and "pains au chocolat." The flowers are now brown and shriveled, but I still have them tucked away in a scrapbook.

The days were passing so swiftly, I was beginning to feel like a native. Everyone seemed happy, even the gendarmes and street sweepers. High heels clicked on the sidewalk as laughing, beautifully dressed women passed by. Hank sat across from me, reading the Paris edition of the *New York Herald Tribune*. One morning, he pointed to a cartoon featuring a couple about our age standing on a busy Paris street. The man was telling his wife to not be surprised if a few French girls recognized him. "Remember," he says, "the war's been over five years and they were mere children when I knew them."

"Did I ever tell you about Ginny?" Hank teased. "She wasn't much taller than you. It was in February of '46 when Hackenberger and I took the electric train to Versailles. We noticed a couple of cute Canadian CWACS (we called them 'quacks') standing near a statue of Louis XIV. They had missed their guided tour, so we volunteered to show them around—even though neither of us had been there before. We were merely extending allied goodwill. We toured the palace, had coffee and doughnuts at an American Red Cross booth, and returned them to their hotel near the Tuileries. The next afternoon, Hackenberger took Myra to the opera while Ginny and I visited a zoo and aquarium.

"It was good to hear her speak good ol' English—not like in Texas, but with a Canadian accent. She used perfect grammar, and if she hadn't used the word 'chaps' so much, I would have thought she was an American. We took Ginny and Myra to the train terminal where they caught the evening express for Bremen, the Canadian occupation zone headquarters. I often wonder whatever happened to Ginny."

"Yes, I remember once you told me you thought Canadian CWACS were of a 'higher class' than American women in uniform. Of course, that was before you knew I had been a Navy WAVE!"

"Well, so much for that conversation," he said, giving me a sheepish look. He began to read to me from Art Buchwald's "Paris After Dark" column. It seems that the main trouble with visiting Europe is that no one really wants to hear about your trip when you get back. Most of your friends, Buchwald says, will be either jealous or bored, so as a public service to his readers, he offers a few hints on travel name dropping—like subtly inserting names in ordinary conversation by saying you picked up a piece of costume jewelry "at the Flea Market in Paris."

I planned to use the technique when I got back to Texas, telling my friends, "it is something I saw at Dior's boutique." Actually, we did attend a mid-season showing by Christian Dior quite by accident. On a bright Wednesday afternoon, after joining a bunch of children at a "Punch and Judy" puppet show, we fed pigeons in a park near the Champs Elysées. A little boy in blue velvet bloomers was pushing his tiny sailboat on the water with a stick. Children were screaming with delight from a merry-go-round. Women in starched white aprons were selling balloons and an organ-grinder was cranking out tinny music while people threw coins to his monkey. A skinny young artist in khaki shorts was standing before his canvas, happily splashing colorful oil paints in modernistic patterns. Then, along Avenue Montaigne, we saw several women in mink coats get out of chauffeur-driven Cadillacs and enter a very ordinary building. A small wooden sign above the door told us it was the showroom of the famous designer, Christian Dior. The women, who appeared to be from elite French social circles, carried white envelopes in white-gloved hands. They were followed by men in top hats and dark suits.

"Is that *the* Christian Dior?" I asked in astonishment.

"Looks interesting. That little sign says the next showing will be at 3 o'clock. Let's go in," Hank said. "I'd like to give it a try."

"But we don't have tickets! Besides, all those women are dressed so properly. Not in wool skirts, ankle socks and loafers."

"Never mind. We'll just ask that woman at the door."

The woman admitted several couples then smiled when Hank said we'd like to go in, too. She studied our passport closely. "Students? From America? Here are two passes. If you hurry, you will probably find seats near the windows."

Fearing thievery, the guards at Dior's were very careful who they admitted to see their fashions. They tried to hide their close scrutiny of every visitor under a heavy mask of graciousness, but I could see and feel the searching eyes of elegantly dressed guards who moved quickly back and forth through the crowd.

Dior's creations were shown in three rather small rooms opening to a wide entrance hall. The century-old building had obviously once been a residence. Gray and blue furnishings were predominant, and a slight touch of "Mist of Dior" floated through the air. Small gold cane-bottom chairs were reserved for the serious buyers, those with special invitations who continued to arrived long after the show began. The confusion and chatter died suddenly with the appearance of the first model and anticipation grew throughout the presentation.

Some latecomers stood on stairways. We had card number ninety-three and were seated on an upper level an hour before the show began. Not long afterward, twenty or so wealthy matrons from South America, a mother-and-daughter combination from the United Kingdom, a young American with a jeweled ring the size of a marble, and several chic Scandinavian women were seated in a roped-off area. Dior used as many as a dozen models—each with bored, unblinking eyes as she moved swiftly among the viewers.

We sat next to Edward, a handsome young American student of fashion design. Hoping to become a "haute couturier," he would not give his full name, as future designers are not too well accepted at showings such as this. He had a thorough knowledge of fabrics, color, trim and balance, and provided us with a continuous commentary on prices, style, and trends. "Prices are outrageous—the simplest frock costs from $150 to $200 and suits go as high as $500," our American friend whispered. Every gown was made of different types of woven fabrics, elaborate embroidery and lace, hand-tucked chiffons and black taffeta. "Silk is block-printed one motif at a time, to give it that exclusive design," Edward told us. "The predominant colors this year are tangerine orange, brown and gray. Dior's fashions will probably be Americanized before the New Look becomes popular in the States."

Edward assured me that in America, silhouette cigarette-slim skirts of the forties would become a bit wider than the French version. "The only thing that changes through the years in women's fashions is the price tag," he said, "especially if it has the flashy touch of being a 'Dior Original.'"

What a wonderful way to end our visit in Paris! Sunday evening we worshiped at the tiny British Methodist Church and then joined a small group for tea and cakes in another hall. It was like a family reunion, as Hank introduced me to several families he remembered. We left Paris the next day for a week with the Grillets before beginning our bicycle journey.

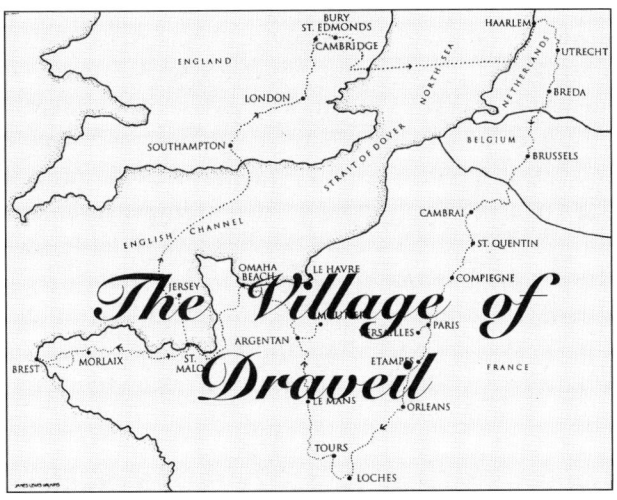

*W*e loaded our few pieces of luggage and the bulky blue camera box and typewriter on a rattling old bus that would let us off in front of Mary's house in Draveil. It was rather sad to watch the Eiffel Tower fade into the distance.

"Paris is more than two thousand years old and still as busy as ever," Hank said in a husky voice. "The picture was not so bright a few years ago. Great art collections were still in storage when I was first here, and there wasn't the wonderful fragrance of spring flowers. Everyone was still feeling the effects of that Saturday morning in August of 1944 when their freedom was finally returned."

Hank described the Paris he remembered, where streets were still barricaded with paving stones, wrecked automobiles, old bedding, gratings and fallen trees. The French felt that if the Germans wished to attack, they would make them pay heavily. The buildings where Germans sought refuge were first assaulted under machine gun fire, then with captured tanks. Place de la Concorde was scarred by bullets and blackened by flames until the German staff surrendered, little by little. The last building to be freed was the Senate, where Luftwaffe headquarters had the most extraordinary defenses of blockhouses and underground passages. Tons of explosives were stored there and more than twenty Frenchmen were tortured or shot during the last seven days. Finally, the gates to the city were opened and General Leclerc's troops and men from General Bradley's American forces marched in an uninterrupted stream, lost in an ocean of joy. Paris was free at last! However, some GIs who marched down the Champs-Elysees on that day died in combat less than forty-eight hours later as war continued in the northeast.

The Grillets' home was built of soft shades of gray stone. Our bus stopped at a wide gate along a brick wall which separated their quiet pebbled courtyard from the bustling noises outside. Mary and the children rushed out as we got off the bus. M. Grillet was more reserved and waited quietly in the doorway. Our luggage was placed at the foot of the stairs and Mary hurriedly made a pot of tea.

Evening passed quickly and I anxiously awaited a real bath upstairs in their long narrow tub balanced on fat little legs. How-

The Grillet family had "adopted" Hank when he was at Orly Field in 1945.

ever, a limited amount of hot water came from a small water heater, slightly larger than a fire extinguisher, that hung high on the wall. We didn't know until later that the Grillets had given us their small bedroom with its beautiful antique bed, and the girls moved to the attic while Jean slept on the couch in the living room. I was quite warm on the fluffy mattress, but the down comforter was hardly long enough to cover Hank's legs.

Sunday was Market Day, a festive affair very much like the outdoor markets along the Mexican border. Hank carried Mary's basket from stall to stall, first to the bakery, then to the pork butcher, and finally to the beef market. Mary said that they did not buy much from the fruit and vegetable carts that lined the center of the wide street because most of their needs came from their own garden. Vendors anxiously waved their wares for everyone to see: clothing, fabrics, kitchen utensils and toys. Most things were much less expensive than they had been in Paris.

Sunday afternoon, Hank walked with M. Grillet across town to the garage where he kept his vintage automobile. They brought the car back and we all drove to Fontainebleau, sixty kilometers southeast of Paris. The palace gardens there, geometric in design, had been modeled centuries ago by Louis XIV to suit his classical taste. Fontainebleau had served as a royal hunting preserve for many years, but now was only a deep forest with soft green wood ferns mixed with an abundance of wildflowers. After strolling through the magnificent chateau and having tea at a nearby pâtisserie, we attended a French movie. They said it was a comedy-mystery, but the "mystery" for me was not in the film, but the rapid clip of the French language. I didn't understand a word!

Everything was blooming in the Grillets' long, narrow garden, enclosed on three sides by a tall stone wall extending back from the house. From June until December, this tiny space provided most of their fruit and vegetables. It rains so often they did not use garden hoses, but sometimes in dry weather they had to carry buckets of water to the plants. A large black pot used for washing clothes was sitting on a few bricks near the back wall, looking very much like a barbecue grill. Mary said that in France, the whole animal is cooked on a spit over an open flame, "from whiskers to tail." Fortunately, I did not have to show her how we did it in Texas.

The kitchen smelled of freshly ground coffee and new paint when we went downstairs to fix breakfast on Monday. The wood

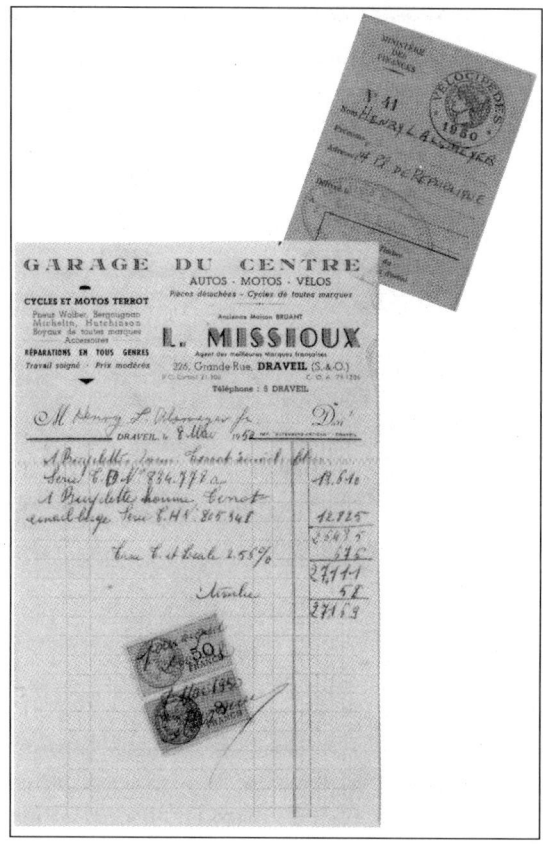

Receipt for the "bicyclettes," two for only
27,169 francs!

stove and a two-burner hot plate for "quick things" were both near
the steps to the cellar, which stayed as cool as an icebox. Mary had
to leave early on her bicycle to get to the schools where she taught
English. Imagine, I thought. A woman her age still riding a bicycle!

Hank placed an antique hand-cranked coffee grinder between
his knees and began grinding the dark aromatic beans. After a few
cups of the strong bitter coffee and crisp french bread topped with
real butter, we made plans for the day. First we must go to the Garage
du Centre at 226 Grande Rue—"automobiles, motos, velos"—where
we hoped to buy bicycles for less than 15,000 francs each (about $45).

Hank's brown bicycle cost 13,640 francs and mine was 12,125.
There was a 2.25 percent sales tax. Each bicycle had five gears and

was equipped with a friction light, pack rack, bell, tire pump and hand brakes. They had standard handlebars and long, hard, narrow seats, but no kick stands. L. Missioux, the agent "des meilleures Marques Françaises," explained how to shift the chain with a flip of the wrist from the large sprocket to a smaller one. Amazing! I had never seen anything like it.

I had never actually owned a bicycle, although years before my sister got one for Christmas and let me ride it occasionally. My toes had hardly touched the ground, and I fell often, for there were no sidewalks. I remembered how most streets were made of hard clay or deep sandy ruts, and I had to put air in the tires every time I rode by the Gulf Station down the street.

"You like?" M. Missioux asked as Hank knelt down to inspect the chains.

"It's a lot fancier than the one I had back in high school when I was delivering the *Houston Post*." he replied.

For me, it was just like Christmas, especially when M. Missioux pushed his cap to the back of his head and a mass of snow white hair fell over his ears. I could have sworn it was Santa himself. Yes, it must be Christmas. I wanted to ride the bicycle right out the front door. Hank carefully counted out the exact amount in francs and we were soon on our way. Only after we had ridden a mile or so back to the Grillet's did I begin to wonder if I could really cycle the winding roads Hank had marked on his maps.

Our first cycling trip was towards Orly Field, ten kilometers from Draveil. To the experienced cyclist, it would have been nothing at all, but for me, the hills seemed steep and the road ever so rough. We picnicked on ham, bread, chocolate, cheese and olives in a garden near the old chateau where Hank had been billeted in 1945. The garden, once beautifully kept, was now overrun with tall grass and an assortment of colorful weeds and wildflowers. In back of the chateau was a private chapel and a five-car garage. There were no other cyclists or hikers, not even a gardener or housekeeper. I pushed aside bits of shrubbery and looked through heavy stained windows. Huge steam heaters and parquet floors were just as Hank remembered.

It wasn't until we returned to the Grillets that we were told the area had been taken over by the Municipality and no one was supposed to enter, much less have a picnic on the lawn.

Americans were still assigned to Orly even though it was now a French civilian airport. We coasted on a rough roadway until we saw an American flag flying and a sign:

ORLY FIELD; MILITARY AIR TRANSPORT SERVICE, HEADQUARTERS FOR THE 6030th AIR BASE SQUADRON AND THE 1632th AIR TRANSPORT WING, ATLANTIC DIVISION

"Orly surely has changed in four years," Hank said as we watched a Trans World Airline plane make a smooth landing. However, Quonset huts built in 1946 and connected by ramps to square frame buildings remained the same. Hank remembered how unhappy everyone was when they had to move from the luxurious chateau to the tiny huts.

"I've spent many an hour waiting out there," Hank said, pointing to a long line of servicemen and civilians boarding buses for Place Vendome. "Looks like the buses still run every half hour."

In 1945, Orly had been the main airfield for transatlantic flights from the U.S., with dozens of C-54s with C-47s, and C-4s used for shorter hauls. Hank had been part of perhaps the world's largest Army Airways Communications System (AACS) Unit.

"Hack and Wilson and I worked six hour shifts with furloughs every three months. I remember Lieutenant Burras and I worked extremely hard to find a way to speed up sending weather material on teletypewriters. It took hours to send weather condition messages even though their value decreased quickly with the passage of time. The information was fed into and out of our center, with transmissions spanning the globe from the east coast of America to India and deep into the Soviet Union and the northern portion of Africa."

It sounded like good duty to me, especially after he told me the French Government gave American servicemen an additional 8500 francs. This practice had ended, however, soon after Hank arrived.

"I remember when a British Halifax heavy bomber landed and parked on that ramp over there," he said, pointing towards a nearby hangar. "It was a British Royal Air Force plane armed with machine guns. The bomb bays weren't too deep, but quite long compared with B-17s. The crew was returning from a practice bombing mission over Italy but stopped here when their radio conked out. One pilot had to admit, however, that a base near Paris was not a bad place to spend the weekend.

"I was fascinated by the traffic of so many kinds of aircraft out on the tarmac," Hank continued. "We could never tell what we would see. They even built a VIP Lounge for brass and gold braid that arrived. One C-54 bore the name of Sunflower II, and had a five-star general's insignia painted on the tail fin. General Eisenhower had sent a general to represent him when former President Hoover arrived. TWA began flying Lockheed Constellations into Orly Field not long after the war, making it the aerial gangplank for both civilians and the military between the States and France. It was a strange looking passenger plane with three tail fins. Before long, everyone will be flying to Europe instead of twenty-one days on a freighter like we did."

Hank was anxious to find the long wooden weather communications building. Most of the system had been removed, but Hank visited two members of the French Office National de Météorologie that he had worked with, then we walked around until we located the grave of an unknown Nazi German soldier who had been buried near the end of a row of huts. The grave was still there. "Dem Unbekannten Soldat" were the simple words carved into the wooden cross erected by Allied forces.

On our way back to Draveil, we stopped at the home of the French family who "adopted" one of Hank's buddies, Art Wilson. Our French/English conversation was rather limited, however, especially with the grandpère. "Répétez s'il-vous plait?" was "répétezed" frequently.

Mary arranged for us to stay in a small apartment in the courtyard behind her neighbor's house. It was more like a box, with one room atop the other, and WC with a very cold shower in a tiny area nearby. Mme. Bruneteau was a large, friendly widow who worked for the postal service. She lived with her teenaged daughter, Ellen, and "Muffatt," her little white terrier. Also living there was her friend Ramona, who worked at the TransAtlantic Telephone Exchange in Paris and spoke excellent English. Mme. Bruneteau wouldn't let us pay for our room, but had one request: she wanted Hank to take a photograph of the Post Office where she worked.

We became familiar with the shady winding streets of Draveil, a community of several thousand persons, and felt quite at home as we cycled about. A few days after we were settled, Mme. Bruneteau invited us to dinner—and what a meal! First we had an aperitif in dainty glasses. On the table were rows of crystal in all sizes: sparkling burgundy was served in bell-shaped glasses and liqueur in thimble sized glasses. By the end of the evening, it didn't seem to matter whether we were speaking French or English!

"How can Americans eat a full meal in only a thirty minute lunch break?" Ramona asked as she brought water from a hand pump outside. "In France, we do not eat—we *dine*. We have equal comfort from a simple omelet as we do to this meal Mme. Bruneteau has prepared." I had no answer.

Mme. Bruneteau was busy preparing fish on a tiny wood stove in her kitchen. "I am preparing this meal like they do in Normandy, with cream sauce and capers," Mme. Brunteau said proudly. This was followed by a main course of veal and ham rolled around hard boiled eggs and cooked in a roaster. She served a thick "floating island" dessert surprisingly like the custard my mother used to make.

During the first week of our stay, Mary took us to the schools where she taught. The children sat at double desks and seemed more studious than American pupils. Their day began at 8:30, included a two-hour lunch break, and ended at 4:30, sometimes followed by a two-hour supervised study period.

"We enroll kindergarten children as early as two years of age. This is the result of the number of 'war babies,' who make up one-fourth of our 600 pupils," said Mme. Yvonne Raquet, the head mistress. Before receiving a baccalaureate degree, students are given final examinations covering the entire four years of study. This includes foreign language, advanced physics, mathematics and history, as well as electives. Certificates are also awarded to a large number of pupils who do not take the "bac" but prefer vocational training instead.

"Perhaps French children know a great deal, but unlike students in America, they are required to absorb too much information in too short a time," Mme. Raquet sighed.

At the time of our visit, all teachers worked under the Civil Service. There were no school boards, because the French government's Department of Education supervised all aspects of education. Andre Leygeus, who taught history and geography, told me that he and other teachers are paid by the Republic of France, with an average

Children at Draveil school.

monthly salary of 24,000 francs, about a hundred dollars. They were also provided the use of modern apartments (utilities paid), which were located on school grounds or above the classrooms.

At the schools we visited, little boys wore gray or black pinafore aprons, while the girls wore brightly colored smocks. They went to separate schools. Only men could teach at the boys' schools, except for Mary's special English classes. "This allows more severe discipline, like twisting ears when they are naughty," the history teacher said, smiling.

M. Leygues proudly showed us his new but rather small automobile and said he would love to take us for an afternoon ride. "Except," he apologized, "I have no tires! All automobiles will be sold without tires until the end of a strike at the tire factory." However, he let us borrow his kayak to float the Seine. I was more than willing

A typical French farmer.

to let Hank handle the paddle while I laid back, basking in the sun. Hank had to admit it was a bit more exciting than canoeing as a Boy Scout on the muddy Nueces River above Corpus Christi Bay.

M. Grillet again got his car out of storage and took us to one of France's more modern farms, 650 acres owned by M. Barlet. Most country farmers in France harbor a skepticism of new agriculture methods, so fields are tilled much as they were in medieval times. M. Barlet's farm was different. From outside a thick wall, it looked like all other century-old farms, but inside, a magnificent garden overflowed with fruit trees in full bloom—peach, cherry and apple. Flowers lined a gravel path leading to a very modern house.

M. Barlet and fourteen other progressive landowners began in 1944 a series of experiments and now had a well organized corporation with a full-time manager. Even though experimental farm test plots were quite common with the U.S. Department of Agriculture Extension Service at the time, in France they were conducted entirely by private individuals who felt the need for this type of work after France was liberated. M. Barlet drove us around his rich farmland in his war-surplus Jeep. The terrain reminded me of the Texas Hill Country, but without rocks. Stone buildings were attached to a thick

One of France's progressive farms.

Mary Grillet greets a friend at M. Barlet's progressive farm.

wall, marking off a prominent section of the village of Harguerutie, an hours' drive from Paris.

"We usually produce eight tons of potatoes a year," M. Barlet said. Hank made careful notes in his journal as Mary translated for us. Eighteen men worked in the fully-equipped workshop and kept the John Deere and other imported farm machinery in top shape. There were only a few head of livestock. Safflowers, plants that produce cooking oil, have turned the fields into a golden yellow blanket with a background of softer colors of wheat dancing in the wind. Mme. Barlet chattered happily—in French—as she served pastries and tea in beautiful china cups.

Before returning to Draveil, we visited two elderly gentlemen named Austermeyer. They were waiting for us in the garden of their magnificent chateau overlooking the Seine Valley. The tip of the Eiffel Tower was visible on this clear day. The two wiry old men were born in Philadelphia but had lived in France for decades. The older brother worked at the Paris American Legion and claimed to be the first American volunteer in the French army during World War I. "That was because I knew the colonel," he said proudly. They were a remarkable pair.

Soon we would begin cycling over the fertile countryside of the Loire Valley that for more than a thousand years had bound Paris with rivers and filled the area with palaces, abbeys, parks and cathedrals. But first, we wanted to cycle about sixty-five kilometers to Versailles, which both Hank and his father remembered well— from two different wars. Hank mentioned the irony of crossing the Atlantic with his troop movement aboard the former passenger liner SS *George Washington*, the same ship that in 1918 had carried President Wilson to Europe following "the war to end all wars."

The palace at Versailles was one of the most regal of all the royal edifices, with a charming, rather sleepy sort of historical amnesia. We returned through several very old villages hidden in deep green valleys. Near Villacoublay was an old but important airport used by the German Luftwaffe and later bombed repeatedly by Allied aircraft. This was the first of many wartorn areas we would encounter.

During our last few kilometers, Hank rolled off ahead of me, anxious to return to Draveil and study his maps one last time. But I stopped for a few minutes, standing in the tall grass beside a seldom-used road, hypnotized by the most amazing pale blue sky I had ever seen. Clouds seemed to turn pink around the edges at the slightest provocation, then suddenly disappear.

"Hee-Haw!" I called, but my voice faded away in the silence of the field. It was the most magnificent solitude I've ever experienced. My head almost burst with visions of hills to climb, palaces to visit, strangers to meet. But I knew nothing would compare to the peace I'd just felt.

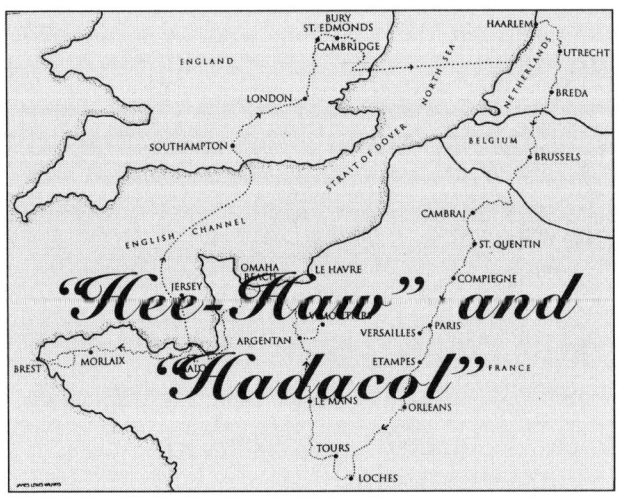

"Hee-Haw" and "Hadacol"

$\mathscr{G}$o just as far as your legs will carry you," Mary said like an old mother hen worrying about her chicks. Mid-afternoon on the eighth day of May, we stored our leather suitcases and portable typewriter with Mme. Bruneteau. We must have been a strange sight. A worn canvas saddle bag borrowed from Mary loosely over the rear wheel of Hank's bicycle and a large blue metal box filled with camera equipment and other odds and ends tied to the rack above. I carried a wicker basket with a few clothes and sweaters, and chocolate, cheese and bread for a couple of days.

Hank spent several hours studying his thick copy of *Le Guide France, Publications du Pneu Michelin des hôtels et restaurants, bonnes tables, spécialites, vins de pays, plans de villes and mécaniciens.* He had already bought several Michelin maps and carefully marked winding back roads connecting tiny villages one to another, like thread from a needle. Mary suggested we stay at inexpensive one-star hotels rather than youth hostels that required separate sleeping quarters. We had never before seen restaurants identified in guide books by

60

symbols of tiny crossed forks and hotels with WC/bath and tiny automobiles. Then there were the asterisks. Four of them indicated the most expensive. Actually, we didn't stay in places listed in the guide but at small family-owned facilities. Hank seemed to be carrying the whole universe in his pockets. For me, maps were only an abundance of distortions and symbols, lines and dots in various shades of tiny blue and yellow wiggly lines showing winding roads. These were overlaid by deep red lines of the main highways. Wide wavy lines marked boundaries of wooded areas, and across Normandy, cities that suffered severe damages during the war were circled in red.

In a few days, Hank had accumulated even more detailed sectional maps of the Loire Valley as well as maps of Normandy and Brittany, 1 cm per 2 km. We sometimes cycled from one edge of the map to the other within a day. This would have been unthinkable in

The wonderland of France.

*One of Hank's maps, "routes et grandes
curiosités."*

Texas, a state so large and odd shaped that most maps cut the
Panhandle off and placed it in a space above Big Bend. Eventually,
Hank added a Shell Oil Company *Wegenkaart van Nederland* and a
Pneu Michelin map for *Amsterdam Bruxelles Paris, Hollande-Belgique-
Luxembourg-Nord de France.* The Amsterdam map listed places of

"Grandes Curiosities," which so aptly describes Hank's curious nature! Of course, we also bought maps of England and central London. It was comforting to know that in England distances were measured in miles and highway signs were written in English. Maps of Normandy and Brittany were scattered with numerous "Montées-Descentes"—hilly with descents—but the Netherlands were flat like the coastal area of South Texas, with even fewer trees.

Hank named his tan bicycle "Hee-Haw," for the familiar bray of a Texas burro. My blue bicycle was "Hadacol," a potent over-the-counter medication for the aging syndrome. If Hank charged ahead of me over a hill or I had trouble in city traffic, I could call out "HEEE-HAAAW. . ." and wait for his echo, "HADA-C-O-L-L-L-L." Bystanders no doubt considered us crazy Americans, and maybe we were!

We cycled most of that first afternoon under a low hanging shelf of dark clouds that changed intensity at frequent intervals. Asphalt bicycle paths along narrow roads were relatively smooth, and with great effort, we slowly pedaled single file the first few kilometers. French cyclists would swish up suddenly behind me, ring tinkling bicycle bells and quickly vanish over the next incline. Sometimes I forgot to move over to let them pass, but they waved and laughed anyway. On one steep incline, a cyclist breezed uphill quite easily with the help of a small putt-putt motor connected to his back wheel.

Near the edge of a little tree-lined village, a group of true racing cyclists wheeled by relentlessly, weaving in and out among the pedestrians like scared jackrabbits. Hunched over handlebars, they whizzed through the village. We were soon caught in a frightening din of buzzers, horns and ringing bicycle bells. Villagers hurried off the narrow cobbled street, shouting "Allez! Allez!," and I thought the villagers were actually cheering for us! The cyclists squeezed into fleeting, shifting spaces at breathtaking speed. I realized we were caught right in the middle—like being in the eye of a hurricane! We were finally able to pull over near a pâtisserie to let them pass. When the cyclists were out of sight, the crowd waved and whistled even more, but this time it *was* for us. A jolly man in a white apron motioned us into his bakery for tea and several curious villagers followed, laughing and talking all at once. I wish I could remember the name of the village.

Low hanging clouds marked the leading edge of another rain storm. It turned bitterly cold and then several line squalls passed over, creating the most fascinating cluster of bluish stratus clouds for several minutes. It was a mixture of color only God could have created. We continued to Etampes and stopped for the night at Hôtel l'Escargot. Most buildings had grayish green moss hanging from their shaggy roofs and were built flush to the street. Despite the cold weather, a flower or two bloomed in neat little window boxes in front of every home. The 300-franc hotel room had a lavatory and a bidet with WC down the narrow hall.

We had our first taste of meat and potato potage (soup) at a little family restaurant. I thought of how shocked mother would be if she knew that, like the Frenchmen at the next table, we sopped it up with bread. For dessert, they served "cassolette," apples wrapped in pastry before baking. Despite the cold winds, we joined a small crowd outside to watch a group of children play a game similar to Mexican piñatas. One blindfolded child, wildly swinging a stick, tried to hit a clay pot hanging by a rope from a tree. When the pot was broken, bags of flour, toys and trinkets fell to the ground and the children laughed and screamed. One pot contained a little white rabbit which children followed as it scampered away.

We left early the next morning, cycling sixty-six kilometers of well maintained roadways across gentle rolling hills. It was a lovely time to cycle, for the day began with such freshness and tranquil strength. We passed several carts and wagons and a few cyclists, but no automobiles. Orleans left no special impression on me except for the few minutes we stopped to watch several stonemasons repair the Cathedral of St. Croix, which had been damaged during the war. Before crossing the Loire at Beaugency, we changed to a less-traveled road towards Chambord. The Loire River is something of a Mason-Dixon Line for France. A short distance to the south are grape vineyards and farther south, orange trees and olive groves. To the northwest, Brittany is perched precariously on a jagged peninsula jutting into the Atlantic. It was here in the reflections of tall willowy birch trees that I began to realize how difficult it is to comprehend the ancient history of the Loire valley.

When I think of "ancient," I ordinarily think of the little town in South Texas where I grew up. The area below the Nueces River was generally poor, sterile sand with only a scattering of mesquite trees on the barren land. It was literally "empty space" before the coming of the railroad, followed by the arrival of settlers including my grandfather, a horse-and-buggy doctor. I remember hearing Texas Rangers tell about the early raids of Pancho Villa, the Mexican "bandido." But that sandy country along Los Olmos Creek is home to me. The creek is usually dry, but when it rains enough, water flows eastward into Baffin Bay and then the Laguna Madre and on to the Gulf. In the early days, Falfurrias was the last stopping place between San Antonio and the Rio Grande Valley. Even the railroad track ended there.

We stopped at a small bank in La Croix to change a few travelers checks into francs. There was an additional twelve percent tax paid to the government. After a lunch of cheese and a bit of local wine, Hank convinced me that the best way to visit this garden of France would be to stay off the main highways and take the less traveled roads on the southern bank of the Loire. He had read that for three centuries, the area was occupied by the Romans who turned

An example of Loire Valley architecture.

the river into one of France's greatest waterways. The evolution of the historic valley's châteaux began in the feudal conflicts of the eleventh century, passed through the rise of the Plantagenets and reached full bloom during the Hundred Years' War with the appearance of Joan of Arc during the fifteenth century. Even though the valley was delightfully flat, the roads were quite rough, and nuts and bolts jolted from my bicycle. I soon became quite an expert with pliers, wrench and air pump.

Many villages had curious winding streets where, with sufficient imagination, I suddenly fancied myself living in the Middle Ages. High to one side of the road were steep cliffs topped with castles clustered around great courtyards. Fortresses perched on rocky plateaus, enclosed by walls eight to twelve feet thick. Farther westward in the valley was an old Italian style castle with lavish ornamentation. During World War II, it had been hit by German bombs and later riddled by small caliber rounds of ammunition that caused irreparable damage.

Oddly enough, during the first few days, I made scant notes of our cycling. Everything was so unreal, like what Alice in Wonderland felt when she climbed through the Looking Glass. However, I still have sharp memories of our leisurely detour to Chambord, where every corner was a sight of jolting beauty. Its construction dates to 1519, the year the Spanish conquered Mexico. The chateau is built like a fortified castle on a flat surface, with each side more than the length a football field. Its imposing height, completed after many years, looked like a huge stone cube flanked by four strong towers. Two entrance halls crossed at the spiral of a beautiful winding staircase.

We found a nice little hotel for 400 francs, memorable for its colorful commodes. We left early the next morning to visit the second chateau, this one in Blois. The castle's architecture consists of various styles dating from the Counts of Blois, the original builders, and later Charles d'Orleans, Louis XII, Francois I, and Gaston d'Orleans, brother of Louis XIII. Each architect seemed to want to add something different. As an afterthought, the brick facade of Louis XII includes a great stairway built on the exterior of one wing. Its warmth contrasts, however, with the later stone construction of the Francois I wing, built between 1515–1524.

We cycled along the northern bank of the Loire to reach Amboise, which looked like most other old castles although histori-

The "cradle of the French Renaissance."

ans describe it as "the cradle of the French Renaissance." The guide told us that in 1492 young Charles VIII returned from what is known as the Naples Campaign with a crew of some twenty workmen and told them to "build it in the Italian style." For a time, it was the home of Leonardo da Vinci and probably marked the beginning of the great movement which transformed French art, even though most of the castle remains Gothic. The Italian influence appeared only in certain areas. World War II resulted in some damage, but fortunately, most of the castle had been restored by the time we visited in 1950.

Springlike weather prevailed during the afternoon until we reached a strikingly beautiful chateau which historians say had nothing to do with wars and fortifications, but was built to the desires of a beautiful woman. Catherine Briconnet died before she could occupy it and her son, Antoine Bohier, used it to pay off an alleged debt of his dead father. Chenonceau's most striking feature is an outgrowth of a bridge that spans the wide River Cher, replacing an earlier castle tower that had been built on the site of a mill. In the middle of the sixteenth century, the bridge was ordered by the famed Diane de Poitiers, the mistress of Henry II, and soon the chateau became filled with stories of intrigue, love affairs and politics. Her authority was later swept away when Henry II was killed and control passed to Catherine de Medici, who built a lovely gallery atop the bridge so she could look down onto the beautiful river below. The gallery is still filled with fine furniture, statues, ornaments and wall hangings from her native Italy.

Southward another twenty-six kilometers was the beautiful Indre River valley. We had a bit of trouble buying lunch supplies because most businesses in France seem to close on Mondays. After lunch, we visited Loches, our final chateau. It contrasted starkly with the peacefulness of Chenonceau. The guide proudly explained the history of the stronghold begun almost a thousand years ago atop a rocky plateau. Thick walls enclose Loches, and there was a great feeling of force and power, but this suddenly changed to horror as we toured the dungeon. The stronghold served at times as a prison. The guide showed us through the dungeon where Cardinal de la Balue, prime minister for Louis XI, had been kept prisoner. De La Balue had devised a barred cell so small no human being could stand up or lie down and ironically, was himself held prisoner in it for twelve years.

The round tower of Loches contained the beautiful tomb of Agnes Sorel, a celebrated favorite of King Charles VII during the fifteenth century. At one time, it had been placed in Saint-Ours, a truly romanesque church dating to the twelfth century. After the church was mutilated during the French Revolution, the tomb was transferred to the round tower of Loches, where it remains today. Atop the tomb is a life-size figure of a woman lying down with two angels at her head. At the feet are two ewe lambs, signifying her name, "Agnes."

We finally arrived at Les Ormes and had no difficulty finding the home of M. and Mme. Mercusot where we planned to camp out for a few days. They had two prewar children as well as two postwar boys, Claud and Pierre. They offered to sail with us in their small boat on the Vienne River but it rained too much. They had put up a sturdy canvas tent, the same one in which Mary Grillet and her children stayed during the worst days of the war, close to a crumbling wall around the Mercusots' grand old house. The tent was quite large.

Hank could *almost* stand up in it. Mme. Mercusot provided a two-burner gas stove with a portable butane tank, pans and dishes.

The butcher at the village market gave me a puzzled look as I spent several minutes studying his wide assortment of cheeses—Cheddar, Camembert, Brie, Munster and many others. He waited patiently until I finally chose one or two, and Hank counted out the coins. On our way back to the tent, the spring mist suddenly turned to extremely cold showers. Crackling thunder and webs of lightning made graceful ballet dances across the sky. I had to prepare our meal inside the tent instead of under the grape arbor as Mme. Mercusot suggested.

On our last night in Les Ormes, Mme. Mercusot invited us to dinner. The limestone floor in her kitchen was worn in places and a huge fireplace covered the stone wall. Pans were suspended over hot coals for heating water. A small butane tank sat on the floor providing fuel for two hot plates. The pantry opened to narrow cellar steps and near the door was a bucket filled with water from a pump outside. Mme. Mercusot spoke very little English, but we got along quite well. The meal was very formal and very delicious. We had strange conversations in broken French and English and much sign

It's a long way from Texas . . .

language. Several different wines were served throughout the meal and as the candles burned low and coals in the fireplace began to flicker, Mme. Mercusot brought tiny crystal glasses for her special homemade cassis—a brandy made with black currants from her garden. I lifted my glass and closed my eyes before taking a small sip. The flavor came through first, then milliseconds later, a roar hit my brain with an unmitigated force. My tongue, the inside of my mouth, and my lips were engulfed in wild conflagrations. I looked quickly at Hank. He had swallowed the whole thing! In one gulp! His forehead began to sweat and his eyes watered. He blinked and sat there, frozen. I think I heard Mme. Mercusot say something like, "Pardon, M. Henri? You like?"

The next morning it took an hour or so to pack our things and pump air into my tires. We cycled—or rather, pushed—our bicycles up a steep hill for seven or eight kilometers, then it began to rain. Hard. Lightning arced to the ground as clouds angrily circled above us. Hail the size of tremendous golf balls peppered down around us and turned the narrow road into a slick sheet of hailstones. The lightning was awesome, and we were the perfect target for it. Against all rules in the Boy Scout Handbook, we took shelter under a lone tree at the top of the hill.

Across the road, as if by magic, a dour old farmer appeared at the door of his small stone cottage, well aware of how severe the storm might get. He waved his arms frantically and motioned us to his dark musty hut. Lightning and thunder cracked even louder as we hurried to place our bicycles along bales of hay in a small cow byre adjoining the kitchen. It was so close, two cows actually watched with big brown eyes every move we made. It may not have been hygienic but it was comforting, like being in a manger. I stood near a pot-bellied stove that gave out a warm glowing heat. The old man's cot was covered with a worn quilt, and a small table and chair sat firmly in the center of the room. The stone floor smelled of lye soap. He stood there shaking his head, his hands in the pockets of his baggy pants, then pulled the wooden shutters together, making the room dark as pitch. We are from America, I told him. No response. *Texas!* Still no response. It became dreadfully quiet.

We waited. And waited. Only the cows outside made any noise. When the hailstones quit falling and shutters opened again to a dark cloudy sky, I noticed the old man's weathered hands, roughened by hard work in good rich earth. He probably lived alone, a man who had endured both wars and floods. He shook his head slowly as he surveyed his vineyard. The future didn't look bright, for the well-cultivated earth was scarcely visible under a blanket of hailstones. Low-growing lush green vines heavy with tiny grapes were bent to the ground by the wind and rain. Rumbling thunder became more distant and an early May breeze chased away dark clouds before sunlight filled the sky once more. A fine mist created beautiful reflections of the sun, suddenly transforming each drop into prisms of color. Storm clouds were soon replaced by concentric bands of a rainbow, and we were finally on our way again. We never knew the man's name. We will never pass his way again. But he will be long remembered, this old man with the roughened hands and generous heart.

The weather got even worse near St. Maure-Noyart. We gave up cycling and boarded a suburban train for Tours where we had to wait in the depot until almost midnight for a connecting train to Argentan. Hank noted in his journal that we arrived at 6:14 A.M. Exactly. Our bicycles weren't unloaded until much later, giving us time for a leisurely breakfast at a small café near the rail station. Rough-looking men in baggy denim pants and black woolen caps laughed and talked at a nearby table as they mixed calvados—a ferocious brown dry apple brandy—with their lukewarm coffee! Hurriedly, they threw a few coins on the counter and left, taking the noise with them.

We unloaded our bicycles and cycled thirty kilometers to Vimoutiers. Wrecked army vehicles of varied sorts lay along the ditches, ugly and forgotten, surrounded by an abundance of wild yellow iris. Thoughts of coasting down the last steep hill to Vimoutiers gave me strength to push the last few kilometers uphill. As we got closer, we could see that the center of the peaceful little village had been completely demolished. Not much was left but rubble and deep holes filled with mud and stones.

It began to rain again.

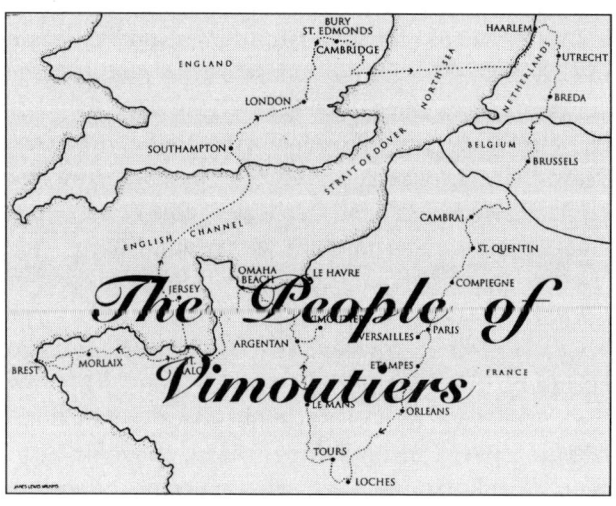

The People of Vimoutiers

*B*efore we left Texas, a member of the philanthropic organization Pilot Club International in Dallas had asked if we would visit Vimoutiers, a small village the club had "adopted" soon after World War II. We found Vimoutiers to be an interesting little village of about 2,000 persons, lying peacefully in the rolling countryside east of Caen in Normandy. It first became visible from a bridge about four or five kilometers away. We stopped while Hank studied his maps and made a note in his journal that Vimoutiers is located in Orne, exactly 125 miles west of Paris and about 75 miles from the English Channel.

Through a misty sky was a beautiful Christmas-like scene of tiny houses around a magnificent old church with a rugged steeple piercing through heavy thick clouds. As we continued toward the village, however, it was obvious that the center of town had been heavily bombed and streets were no longer neatly cobbled, but instead filled with potholes and debris. The area was now peaceful, but its charm had been shattered about 8 A.M. on June 14, 1944, only eight days after D-Day. Bombers of our own Ninth Air Force flew out of the morning mist to dump load after load of bombs on the town. It was purposeful and accurate bombing, but it turned out to be one of the great tragedies of war. In the fifteen minutes of bombing, 250 persons were killed and many more maimed and wounded; the town's main buildings were destroyed. Incendiary bombs started fires which burned for several days and many buildings that had been left standing were gutted by fire. The Ninth Air Force bombed Vimoutiers because it was given information—via carrier pigeons released by the Germans—that the village was the storage spot of large amounts of their ammunitions soon to be turned against the Allies in battle not far away. This was not true, but when the truth was learned, it was too late. Vimoutiers was in ruins.

My friend in Dallas said that in 1949, Pilot Club International began offering aid to the people in the brave little village. We found the courage and determination of the people to be inspiring. A few undamaged stone block buildings had been left standing in the town. Dangerous utility wires still hung loosely from tall thin posts along the road. Temporary wooden structures had replaced centuries-old buildings. As we cycled over the creaky wooden bridge, I could see

Temporary barracks-like structures in Vimoutiers.

that despite the day's rain, it was business as usual for villagers. Boys in short pants, bulky sweaters and high boots splashed merrily along the street carrying long loaves of bread. A woman pushed an old baby carriage filled with odds and ends to sell. The people of Vimoutiers did not sit back to wait for help in restoring their town. They salvaged from the rubble all that could be used, and with great ingenuity erected temporary buildings for both individual families and the community as a whole. In the village square there stood a great statue of Mme. Marel, who at the end of the eighteenth century invented a soft gold cheese called Camembert whose name comes from a nearby village. The bombs had not moved her, but she stood there headless, a grim reminder of those few minutes when bombs rained destruction to all below.

The mayor's office, in a barracks-like frame structure with floors that swayed as we entered, was easy to locate amid the rubble. The first thing I noticed was a plaque for the most coveted of all French decorations, the Croix de Guerre. The citation recounted the village's courageous behavior during both the war and Germany's occupation; its suffering during all of the tests to its spirit and its faith in peace and in the future.

Mayor M. Gavin was out, but after we explained the purpose of our visit, the city clerk—who fortunately spoke a bit of English—accompanied us to the home of Dr. and Mme. Boullard a few blocks away. They lived in a stately red brick home, the only one left standing to the north of the town square. Other buildings were literally flattened for nine or ten blocks in all directions. As he introduced us to Mme. Boullard, the clerk explained that both she and her physician husband worked closely with the Pilot Club, as well as participating in other civic activities.

"Only yesterday, several Pilot Club officials from Washington, D.C. drove out from Paris. It takes only two hours," Mme. Boullard said. I looked at Hank. Only two hours? Then I remembered that it took us longer because we stopped in Les Ormes and then had to board the train because of rain and rough cycling. Our route was slower and more difficult, but it made me more mindful of the beautiful country south of this area that faced almost total destruction six years ago. Mme. Boullard then told us about the lovely old church whose clock-adorned spire had stood watch over the village for centuries. The face of the clock was pockmarked, but the hands continued to tell the time.

Remains of war torn village of Vimoutiers.

"Can you imagine what it was like to attend early Mass on a peaceful Sunday morning and have the ceiling fall on you?" Mme. Boullard asked. "Glass from the windows shattered all around us and when we went outside, we saw our entire village had been blown up and everything was in flames. All of this happened in less than fifteen minutes! As with many other bombed areas, though all around was flattened, our church remained standing, its spires a beacon of hope to those who survived. Unfortunately, we no longer have any musical instruments, not even our beautiful organ." Mme. Boullard almost wept as she told how difficult it is for her music-loving French friends to be without their instruments.

She served tea while her young grandson, Phillipe, played quietly nearby. The little boy in bloomer pants finally whispered something to his grandmother and pointed to Hank. "He wants to know why the tall gentleman from Texas talks so strangely!" I'm sure Mme. Boullard wondered that as well! Phillipe's father, Denis Barois, played a vital part in arranging for Pilot Club International to sponsor the reconstruction of this village, she explained.

Following the bombing, Dr. Boullard, the village doctor and all other physically able men and women rushed to give aid to the

Madame Boullard and grandson, Phillipe.

stricken people. Five of the seven nuns who operated the small hospital had been killed in the bombing. Mme. Boullard showed us the book her husband had compiled in 1948 with a detailed history of the village. He had gathered papers and records confirming that people had lived in the area for twenty centuries, beginning with the Romans. His collection of pictures from before and after the bombing was unbelievable. As the doctor pointed out in listing the war dead, Vimoutiers lost more people in fifteen minutes during a

Shy kindergarten children at Vimoutiers school.

single bombing than they had lost in all of World War I. Europeans must realize, he explained thoughtfully, that the French cannot expect to keep their civilization through another war as destructive as this.

Mme. Boullard walked with us across recently dug drainage ditches, pointing out great vacant holes where buildings had once stood. "Many surprising incidents occurred during the horrors of this war," she said. "One family with twelve children lived in one of the houses that fell during the first wave of the raid. The children crouched under a sturdy dining room table until the last of the bombs had hit. As rescuers went about their tasks in the smoldering debris, these twelve children—in single file—walked out of the rubble, hand in hand. They said that only the night before, their father had warned them that if there was ever a bombing raid, they must take shelter under the sturdy round table." She hesitated, then hardly above a whisper, said softly, "Both of their parents were killed."

We had lunch at a tiny inn where Mme. Boullard introduced us to the owner, who was also the cook. "I took over the business after my mother was killed," he explained matter-of-factly. "The inn was totally destroyed, but life must go on. Slowly and painfully, we will survive." I had not expected the delicious meal he served, beginning with hors d'oeuvres of ham and eggs and followed in quick succession by fish, green salad, cheese souffle, pudding and cookies. Dessert was fruit and coffee!

I would have been content to stay in the warm surroundings all afternoon, but Mme. Boullard wanted us to visit the auditorium, now used as the Town Hall. The Pilot Club had donated over a hundred seats, all bright red plush. Shiny new desks had already been installed in the boys' school, and a door was replaced on a small building to keep it warm for the girls' gym classes. The Pilots also contributed vast amounts of clothing, food and money. The gate to the school for girls was open and children were marching into a small classroom, the taller girls at the front and short ones in back, just like the Navy's WAVES Boot Camp! Their eyes sparkled as they sang and one tiny girl in a tan apron broke away and ran towards me with a handful of wild flowers. When I leaned over to kiss her, she threw her arms around my neck and hugged me tightly. The boys at the school across the street were not so demonstrative, but giggled in typical small boy fashion as we talked to them. Some wore wooden dutch shoes, others had on rubber boots. Many were orphans.

"There were so many wounded people, especially children," Mme. Boullard said. "A bomb would go 'pisst' and a building would disappear. The doctor was quite busy helping the injured at the temporary hospital set up in the Manor House near the Square."

Tales of the occupation of Vimoutiers by the Nazi troops were not pleasant to hear. The events were still vivid in her mind. Their nineteen-year-old son had been killed by the Germans in the woods just outside Vimoutiers. Another son became a member of the French Air Corps. One daughter was a Dominican Nun and the other daughter married a young engineer, Denis Barois, Phillipe's father. He was also in the French Air Corps and trained for three years in the United States. While there, he met the famous author of *Gone with the Wind*, Margaret Mitchell. After he told Ms. Mitchell about this village, it seems the war suddenly gave her life a direction that it hadn't had since the first manuscript of her book had been turned over to the publisher. She volunteered to roll bandages, was a street warden, and like everyone else, coped with shortages of sugar and butter. Through her efforts, Pilot Club International took on this project, carrying out the Club's motto of "True Course Ever." Ms. Mitchell was made an honorary citizen of Vimoutiers in 1949.

The community is most proud of Salle Labertrie, a recreation center where movies are shown twice weekly. Its badly damaged walls and ceilings have been restored and are now filled with a varied assortment of chairs. The ailing boiler provides at least some heat. Today, cattle graze on the rolling plains, and large orchards are being replanted. Peasant women again make linens and fancy embroideries in their homes to be sold throughout France. Inhabitants of this village, just as those in Caen and St. Lo and St. Malo, are working hard to rebuild their homes and centuries-old buildings that hold so much history. Many cities and villages in the Normandy area will have new faces, but the people will remain the same—hard working and thrifty, with many stories to tell children such as young Phillipe. The church still dominates both the scene and the lives of the people in an impressive way.

Hank had seen Frankfurt while in Germany in 1946, but he said it did not compare with the destruction that had taken place here in only a few minutes. The labor, the skill, the genius, the love and the spirit of thousands of ordinary people have all gone into the rebuilding of the church. Cracked walls had been repaired, but church windows remained covered with unpainted boards, shutting out the sunlight and contributing to an old, musty odor inside. Still, it is a place of refuge for these devout people of deep faith.

We left Vimoutiers under very dark clouds but no rain, and with winds at our backs, had moderately smooth cycling seventy kilometers to Caen, arriving long after dusk. The city is considered Normandy's cultural center, and it too is trying to rebuild from the war. I had read somewhere that the stones used to build Westminster Abbey came from the Caen area. The evening we arrived was the beginning of Whitsun or Pentecost, a religious holiday, and all the hotels were filled. We cycled a few kilometers west to a small inn in an old house at a crossroad near Rots. It was almost 9 P.M., but fortunately, daylight hours were lengthening and it was still quite light. They offered us a small clean room—WC outside—for twenty francs. While the woman prepared an evening meal her husband worked on antique farm equipment in the barn and their two small sons tried to harness a big shaggy sheep dog to a cart. It was probably a huge Belgian sheep dog, beautiful and very very patient, and oh so big!

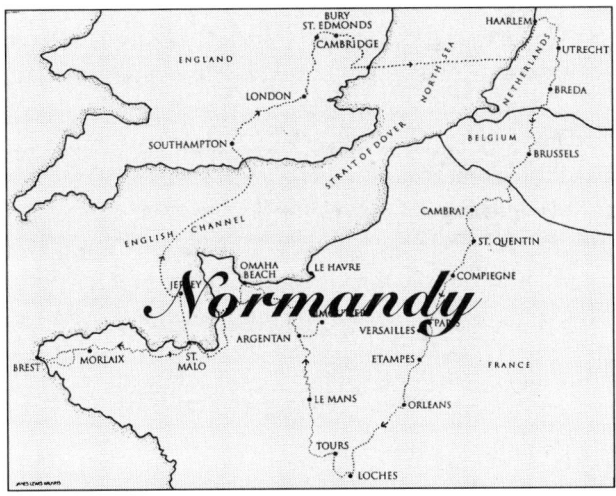

$\mathcal{F}$irst impressions remain with me
the longest. This was especially true in Normandy, as we cycled a
mile or so back from the sea along a road lined with orchards filled
with late winter apples. Farmers were busy at great wooden presses
making their own brew, a sour-sweet acrid cider of great potency.
White cattle blotched with black and brown spots roamed content-
edly in nearby pastures.

Hank marked his maps carefully, for we seldom cycled major
macadam roads, preferring forgotten lanes that eventually ended in
small hidden villages. Around Caen and southwards towards Falaise
and Thury Harcourt and on towards the coasts of Normandy and
Brittany, maps showed many villages circled in red, meaning they
had been severely damaged during the war. In places, the red circles
were as thick measles blotches. Most areas were also distinctly
marked with an abundance of "<< 7% >>," which on our maps
indicated the degree we would ascend. Even though much was lost
during the war, there was still a great deal of beauty. New settlements
had sprung up in every valley. The area was steep and rocky, with

great slabs of granite edging down to deep mysterious gorges looking as if they had been tortured by erosion into strange exotic shapes. Here and there, deep purple colors changed into rose and ocher and shades of yellow.

My legs grew weary as we cycled relentlessly along twisting roads to a village where for seventy francs, we bought enough cheese at the local market to last three days. Each wedge was packed in a little flat round box; soft yellow Camembert with a grayish white rind was my first choice. For another seventy francs, we purchased a bottle of wine, and paid an additional twenty francs for the bottle!

There is nothing better in life than to rest in the shade of a gnarled apple tree while white and gold daisies stir and sway in the strong breeze. The air was thick with scents. I could hardly eat lunch for watching a small herd of cows that had the most curious wide eyes I had ever seen. At first, they ran to the far corner of the field, but before long they began coming closer until finally they were in almost a perfect circle around the apple tree, six pairs of soft bovine eyes sparkling like balls of polished ebony.

After lunch, we cycled westward some twenty kilometers, passing through Bayeux, and turned north towards the shoreline. For many hundreds of years, this part of Normandy had only a few small villages hidden throughout the extremely rough terrain. During World War II, however, it won its spot in history when American

Omaha Beach, six years after D-Day.

blood, valor, raw courage and sheer guts began the fierce D-Day invasion. According to Hank's maps, Omaha Beach was only seven kilometers farther to the west. There, the 2d Ranger Battalion, commanded by Texas's Lieutenant Colonel J. Earl Rudder, had scaled 100-foot cliffs at Pointe du Hoc, destroying gun emplacements which threatened landing sites below. A great deal of history took place near here in June of 1944, when the massive invasion was followed by one of the most spectacular advances of modern warfare.

To the west was also the area where my brother parachuted with the 82d Airborne Division to set up a pre-invasion hospital near Saint Marie-Eglise. He seldom talks of it. Other paratroopers had cut railroad lines, blown up bridges and seized landing fields.

To express their public sentiment following the war, the French constructed the "Voie de la Liberté" (Road to Liberty), a highway marked with stones shaped like German pillboxes and carrying the image of a flaming torch. It is dedicated to the French citizens and their momentous exploits when their Underground finally heard long-awaited D-Day messages. Saboteurs began doing everything possible to make it difficult for the Germans to defend themselves. When Americans arrived, civilian soldiers—both men and women— informed the Allies of every last-minute development on the German side. Whenever the Germans advanced, the French people had already provided Allies with highly organized Underground armies in support.

Overgrown hedgerows blending into the landscape seemed to be a special part of rural life. Most people forget the hedgerows are not formed naturally, but are artificial barriers planted to protect cattle and sheep as well as providing a vital source of free food the whole year around. They also made perfect defensive positions for German troops.

Tiny flowers popped up in rustic areas and thyme, fennel, chives and other herbs peeped out from shady places along the ditches. There were no trees on the grass-covered cliff above the coast. Far below were broad tidal sands, and farther out the rusting hulls of sunken ships and half-sunk barges formed a breakwater some two miles long. Rows of amphibious DUCKS were still visible, some with wheels still in place. Actually, DUCK is the nickname for seven-ton six-wheeled U.S. Army trucks named DUKW: D (1942), U (amphibious), K (all-wheel drive), and W (dual rear axles). Many of these amphibious vehicles, carrying twenty-five or thirty men ashore, overturned in rough seas after hitting underwater concrete barriers placed there by the Germans. Floating piers and a barge or two lay rusting and covered with algae. A lone German pillbox overlooked a bluff, and still visible on the rough concrete wall was the message left by one proud American soldier: KILROY WAS HERE.

Roads once bulldozed up ravines in the cliffs by American combat engineers were now fenced and overgrown with grass. Only a small plaque inscribed in French identified the beach, and another marker had been placed nearby as a memorial to the engineers who died there. It was quiet except for a few tourists and the laughter of small children playing on the beach with their buckets and shovels. They meticulously built beautiful castles of sand, only to look back to see their hopes and dreams washed away by the sea.

It was difficult for me to believe that for fifty miles along these peacefully quiet beaches, Allied troops had waded ashore when the invasion began. I stood there in the brisk wind from the sea, the sun breaking through billowing clouds, and heard the laughter of little children. Will it be this peaceful in fifty years, I wondered. Would D-Day be remembered then?

Nearby was the American cemetery at St. Laurence Sur Mer, a beautiful area atop the bluff overlooking the beachhead. It was peacefully quiet when we arrived the day before Memorial Day, and difficult to realize that only six years before this area had been the scene of days of massive, horrendous combat. White crosses, row upon row, waited patiently to be replaced with marble. One cross had been placed there for a young soldier Hank knew in his Boy Scout Troop No. 52 back home. His fallen friend was an only child whose family name is now buried beneath one of the crosses here in Normandy.

This well-tended cemetery was quite different from the over-grown area of German graves with black crosses visible behind a locked gate. From a slight hill overlooking a village, it appeared to have been constructed hurriedly by Americans as they were leaving the area to pursue other German forces. There was no entrance marker.

We passed through battered St. Lo and bought an assortment of cheeses. A dry goat cheese called Brocciu wasn't too bad, even though it smelled awful. There was a feeling of antiquity in this village, famous for its beautiful copper pots, ash trays, demitasse spoons and many other copper and brass things. Women vendors wore traditionally bright colored red, green and blue dresses with equally colorful scarves wrapped around their heads. They hawked their wares from straw mats on the cobbled street while men shouted enticements from two-wheeled carts. I walked slowly by the vendors, tempted to fill my basket with many treasures, but bought only a pair of tiny crocheted gloves for mother. Hank pushed his bicycle through the noisy hucksters and waited for me at the corner, anxious to cycle another sixty-two kilometers to Calvados By-the-Sea for the night.

The road from Villedieu was relatively smooth but it took another thirty minutes to push our bicycles to the top of a steep incline near Avranches. Hank didn't tell me until later that the altitude increased from ten to over a thousand meters. After buying a camera filter and Kodachrome film, we stopped for magnificently messy, gooey pastries, then continued to a bluff overlooking the Baie du Mont Saint Michel. We had our first glimpse through misty skies of the fabled Mont rising above the vast sands exposed on the tidal flat. We left about 2:30 P.M. and cycled to a lovely inexpensive old mansion not far from the causeway leading to the Mont. Hank wrote in his journal, not about weather or kilometers we had traveled, but that for three consecutive nights we had room number 4, the two following nights, number 24. The kind landlady offered to wash and iron Hank's khakis, but I continued to hang our daily "laundry" on a tight string across our room.

The gray Breton coast to the west stretches far into the horizon and extends more than three miles after high tide. The story of the Mont spans a most curious mixture of geography and history. The exterior is no less remarkable than the interior, especially the narrow bridge reaching from the top of a spiral staircase across to the rest of the church. When we were there, the Mont was threatening to become landlocked once more, due to the modern causeway interfering with the sweep of the tides (which at annual peaks may be more than forty feet).

From the hotel, the Mont, which the French properly call "La Merveille," looked like a fairy wonderland. It is challenging to describe, for over a thousand years of Christian history have been built and impressed into it. Victor Hugo once said of Mont Saint Michel that it is to the rest of France as the Pyramids are to Egypt.

This rock of granite, towering above a sandy stretch of bay that divides Normandy and Brittany, is known as the "Peril of the Sea," or "Saint-Michel-au-Peril-de-la-Mer." Hundreds of years ago water ate up a great forest, tree by tree, bush by bush, until only a rocky islet was left surrounded by the sea at high tide and also by quicksand. The whole western face of the Mont is formed by sheer rocks covered with vegetation. English forces learned during the Middle Ages how deadly these sands could be when combined with tides. Three times they attempted to conquer the Mont but never succeeded.

There is a tangled mixture of geography and history in this rock which rises more than 240 feet above tidal flats. Marshy plains extend far into the distance, forming muddy edges in the bay where farmers extract a sandy substance called tangue. It smells like wet clothes and

Overlooking the bay at Mont St. Michel.

is used for manure. The Mont served as a monastery from the ninth century until the Hundred Years' War, was captured and became a fort, and later housed a monastery again. In 1721, Maurice de Broglie obtained the Mont in exchange for 600 bottles of Burgundy and held it for almost forty years. A small medieval village rests in a girdle of walls almost three thousand feet in circumference. The sea surrounds it all at high tide, but a causeway built later makes it always accessible. A winding cobbled street struggles up the steep granite hill lined with small shops selling very expensive trinkets. Even though the quiet cloister was badly mutilated during the French Revolution, the view remains breathtaking. Wind and rain have worn smooth the few remaining delicate carvings of fruit, ornate flowers and religious scenes.

A small parish church, leaning heavily on the shoulder of the rock, led still more unexpectedly to a tiny cemetery. Some French say that the secret of the Mont's beauty is that everything fits together, having been built by a single group of people with a tradition that has lasted hundreds of years. Others claim, however, that faith built it, the sword defended it, and the state has taken it over.

Hank assured me he was saving the best for last: dinner at Mere Poulard's. Since the seventeenth century, omelets have been made

A thousand years of history . . .

the same way at this small restaurant. Eggs are beaten with a wire whisk for an endless amount of time, then put into a long-handled skillet and cooked over open flames. Omelets, made without salt— "for that toughens it," the waitress said—were also served with tiny red shrimp, so tender we ate shell and all. Sitting in front of a huge stone fireplace and taking the last drop from a bottle of Alsatian wine seemed to bring back vivid memories of Hank's first visit four years earlier and to loosen his tongue enough to share them.

Thanks to special rates for servicemen, he had traveled first class from Paris in a compartment with a produce buyer. Before reaching the Mont, the stranger told him the fascinating history of the area and was repaid with two packs of Hank's American cigarettes. On returning to Paris, Hank was fortunate to share a compartment with a former prisoner in Stalag Luft Two and a French first lieutenant who fought with the 11th Ranger Regiment on the Cherbourg Peninsula.

"They had great stories to tell. It was surely different from the furlough I took later to England and Scotland. I went by boat-train to London, and spent the night at a Red Cross center before boarding the Flying Scotsman. The British must have a rigid rule about not speaking to strangers, for I was in a compartment with five English businessmen all the way to Edinburgh and not a word was spoken! The trip was worth it, though, for I thoroughly enjoyed the beautiful scenery and especially the Scottish family I met when I visited the newspaper office. The editor had a son my age and invited me to dinner and later gave me a tour of Edinburgh."

Hank stretched his long legs in front of the fireplace, absorbing the warmth of the big logs. "It was bitterly cold and quite desolate during my first visit, but I gave the guide my last few cigarettes, and he took me into several areas not usually viewed by tourists."

"Were there any other people here?" I asked.

"Well, yes," he said, hesitantly. "I remember sitting in front of this same fireplace with five lovely young women on leave from an American Red Cross post. The simple pleasure of visiting with young American women was tremendous."

"I'll bet it was! *Five* girls?"

"Yes. It was in front of this same fireplace about four years, three months and fifteen days ago. We were the only tourists and they treated us royally," he teased.

"You? With *five* cute girls?" I repeated.

"That's another story, and it's too late to tell it," he said, putting on his field jacket to leave. We stepped into cold bitter winds coming with the rising tide and mounted our bicycles for the short ride across the causeway to the hotel.

"*Five* girls?" I repeated when we got to our room. Hank only smiled. If I had had my way, he would not have worn clean khakis the next day.

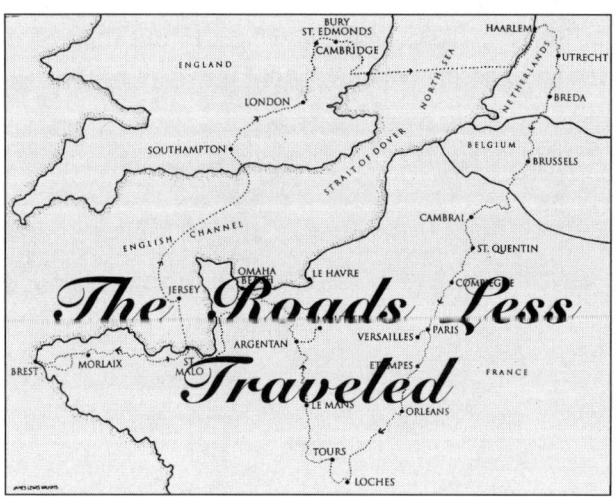

The first day of June. We slowly cycled inland to Pontorson for lunch and then through a few of Brittany's delightful tiny villages that pop up over almost every hill. This unexpected beauty made leaving richly historic Mont Saint Michel a bit easier.

Brittany is much harsher than green fertile Normandy because it has only a thin covering of soil in the fields and more gray rocks than grass. Endless action of the sea has worn the pebbled shoreline into a series of little bays on the sandy wild coast with misty valleys along the edges. Bretons are Celtic in ancestry and their speech bears a relationship to the people in Ireland and Scotland, whose Gaelic language was introduced during the fifth and sixth centuries. The region is one of the most beautiful in France, with the delicate charm of people who seem passionately attached to their native land. In the center of one village, a small group was singing wild discordant Celtic dirges accompanied by a two-man bagpipe. People are proud of their ancient Norman-Gothic cathedrals, and churches have interest-

BANQUE DE FRANCE   **SAINT·MALO** le *1°* *Mars* 19 *50*
(Date de réception de la demande)

DEVISES ÉTRANGÈRES (1) {
DÉLIVRÉES
ACHETÉES
REÇUES A L'ENCAISSEMENT
}

M* H L Alsmeyer .
adresse
titulaire du passeport N°
délivré le 3 14 Janvier 1950 par Washington
1) Rayer la mention inutile   2408 - B. de F. - Imp. J. Vanderperre Paris - SF - 4021 - 1-49 - 120.000

	DEVISES	COURS	DÉCOMPTE	
$	20	369,80	Fr. :	6 925
		–1 %	Fr. :	
		366,30	Fr. :	
Chèque N° B 88586623			C° ou %	
— N°				
— N°				
Billets : Coupures de				
d°				
d°			NET :	6 926

NOTA

Les billets de banque libellés en
ne peuvent être repris au retour de voyage

— qu'en coupures de
— pour un montant maximum de

Il est rappelé qu'avant leur retour en FRANCE, les voyageurs ont la faculté de déposer dans une banque du pays où ils se trouvent, aux fins de rapatriement par virement bancaire, l'excédent des sommes en devises dont ils disposent.

Exchanging $20 for 6926 francs in St. Malo.

ing assortments of saints—for horses, blacksmiths and even for pigs. One saint claims to make frogs croak whenever he wants.

Faint rumbles of thunder were followed by cauliflower-shaped clouds that darkened the sky, but we made good time over relatively flat terrain, arriving at about two o'clock in St. Malo, an important port for crossing to the Channel Islands and Southampton. The streets were very busy and people spoke in strange dialect. The area had suffered greatly from war damages. At the tourist bureau, a clerk gave us several brochures and suggested that we attend a forthcoming "Pardon" at Rumengol.

The vedette crossing the waters to St. Malo's sister city of Dinard was a fascinating piece of technology. It would spin and whirl as it gyrated through port traffic: fishing boats and coastal freighters along a medieval countryside. We cycled west and after a night in Ploubalay, went thirty-seven kilometers to Lamballe in almost three hours. The map of the countryside was filled with an amazing number of "<<" and ">>" denoting steep inclines and descents, but the landscape exhibited very little war damage.

From there, we took the train for the next 110 kilometers to Morlaix, where we had time for a leisurely stroll through the city's interesting mixture of old and new. We had coffee and pastries at the ornate but inexpensive Palais de France, typical of the Queen Ann of Brittany era dating to the fifteenth century. The original staircase, built on the outside wall like the one at the chateau of Blois, spiraled up three or so stories, but was so narrow only one person could climb it at a time.

Captain LeRoux had told us aboard the *Pont L'Evêque* that his family lived in Morlaix, this small city located on one of the many

Viaduct at Morlaix.

estuaries along the northern coast of Brittany. A major trading harbor during the Middle Ages because it is easily accessible to the Channel, it became a natural target for attacks from England as early as 1522. One raid is commemorated in the town's punning motto: "S'il este mordent, mords-les"—*If they bite you, bite them back!* Once a raiding party from England found the town undefended so they looted the houses and drank themselves senseless. When the folks from Morlaix returned from a nearby festival, they massacred the raiders—hence the motto.

At the time of our visit, Morlaix still had a wealth of fine, half-timbered and granite houses where merchants lived. The oldest church, St. Melaine, was built in flamboyant Gothic style and lay in the shadow of the town's famous railroad viaduct. Maritime Morlaix

Along roads less traveled . . .

Abandoned church near Pont Christ Bridge, near Landerneau.

is downstream from the viaduct where the quay, once crowded with merchant shipping, had been given over to small boats. Near Landerneau, we picnicked on the craggy banks of an icy stream near the old "Pont Christ" bridge. Towering above the church was the arch that we had seen from the road. Beautiful, vine-covered walls had large holes like empty eye sockets that once held stained glass windows. Weathered walls stood unroofed but upright, opening to

One of the smaller calvaries at St. Thegonnec.

the beautiful blue sky above. Some of the pillars had been reduced to meaningless grass-covered stumps. Beyond the broken stones stretched a small empty field covered with flowers. The edifice had once been quite large—far different from the small frame churches at home in Texas that tend to topple over during the slightest dust storm. Debris has long since been removed and now a mantle of earth and flowers covers the floor. Strange colorful birds flitted about the mossy rocks, making it one of the most inspirational settings we saw on our entire trip.

Because the terrain became even more mountainous, there was much bike-pushing before we finally stopped to take photographs of a calvary at St. Thegonnec, sixteen kilometers from Morlaix. The fourteen-foot arch-like monument represented the crucifixion with a gnome-shaped figure of Christ on the cross and two thieves nailed to smaller crosses at his side. An angel sat on the shoulder of the thief on the right, the devil on the left. Some of the stone figures had lost their identity through time and weather, but if we had not been so hurried, I am sure we could have identified most of the Biblical stories. Unaware of our presence, a bearded stonemason in a woolen cap knelt with his hammer and chisel, slowly but methodically repairing one granite column. Throughout the countryside we saw smaller, more primitive calvaries from as early as the sixteenth century. Some were crudely made and tilting a bit, but all reached towards the sky like Arizona saguaro cactus.

Large calvary at St. Thegonnec near Morlaix.

We cycled through Landivisiau and Landerneau, arriving at a small hotel in Daoulas by late afternoon. It was a quaint village where some of the older women still wore traditional lace head coverings, long black skirts and wooden clogs. Bretons along the coast are mostly sailors, fishermen or farmers; the townsfolk lean to weaving and are proud of the delicate lace designs they have created. They go about their business in a medieval setting of old houses and gateways along twisting narrow streets. We pedaled slowly and stopped often to touch and enjoy the intricate carvings or wander through the awesome dark, musty churches. Brittany has more than its share of saints, and for most saints, they have special religious Pardons, testifying to their profound religious fervor.

Women in native dress, Brittany.

Early on Sunday morning we joined the villagers to celebrate an ancient Pardon at Rumengol, a little stone church sitting atop a mountain overlooking one of the fingers of the bay at Rade de Brest. This bay encompasses a great hand-shaped area of water that comes together at the neck, called Goulet de Brest. The Pardon turned out to be a fascinating mixture of events. Roads along the last few tree-lined kilometers to Rumengol were narrow and dusty as we followed crowded buses, a few automobiles, and hundreds of other people on foot or pushing their bicycles. Log gates between hedgerows were pulled aside and hucksters collected money to keep our bicycles secure. Ornately-dressed men sold jewelry, candy and handmade gloves along with fruit, sausage, local wines, cider, and strangely enough, rifle targets. One young Frenchman took time out for his morning shave near a small stream; couples made love in secluded corners; and behind nearby hedgerows, a man urinated. Only the older women wore distinctive costumes of Old Brittany—enormous head dresses and collars of stiff accordion pleats that stood out well past their shoulders, elaborate lace stovepipe coiffes, and wooden clogs. Teenage girls dressed in modern fashion but the younger children danced around in gay ankle-length embroidered dresses and small multicolored lace caps. Elderly men seemed to have stepped from a Dickens novel in their maroon velvet waistcoats with silver buttons and jet black ten-gallon flat-topped furry hats decorated with wide satin ribbons and silver buckles.

Once a year the village people celebrate this religious festival to obtain a "pardon" for their mistakes. We arrived as throngs followed their priest in a procession, carrying silver crosses and banners embroidered in gold. They were chanting the "Kantik" which tells the story of Christ coming to Rumengol. Banners hanging between the church and an outdoor sanctuary sported Breton's tongue-twisting inscriptions, "Saenz Mari Pedit Evidomp" and "Gjere Hez en Kantic." The church, like many others we saw in Brittany, had its own elaborate sixteenth century stone calvary. It depicts Christ with two thieves standing on a pedestal and smaller figures below. Lichen covers the carvings that are now corroded by salt air, but the story remains the same. The broader scene, however, was more like a carnival where people laughed and danced under red, green and orange canopies, and spoke strange combinations of French and Celtic. After mass, they spread white tableclothes on the grass and picnicked on wine, bread, cheese, and very spicy sausage.

"Pardon" festival at Rumengol.

At the end of the day, people returned to their homes and tiny Rumengol settled back to being a quiet Breton village. Unlike the local folks who chose to go back down the winding mountain road, Hank chose another route that first turned uphill along a crooked heavily wooded dirt path.

"You don't know where we'll come out, do you?" I finally asked.

"But I *do* know!" he insisted.

"Your map doesn't show any tiny blue lines along here!"

Processional at Rumengol "Pardon."

"This is a shortcut so you can see Brittany's most celebrated calvary, at Guimillau. The road's a bit more narrow than I expected," he admitted.

"But Hank," I said as soon as I caught my breath after huffing my thousand-pound bicycle up and down narrow paths and around mile-high piles of rocks. "Your map shows this as the 'Petit Suisse de France.' That means *little Switzerland*."

"Just wait. It's only a bit farther," he said. Fatigue bogged my mind and body. My legs and spirit began to wobble and I wondered just why I was there.

When we reached the spot, the calvary at Guimillau, it was a bit disappointing in size and beauty, but taking my shoes off to wade in the icy cold headwaters of the Coatoulgach River was worth the detour. We saw a few people who seemed to be living as they did centuries ago. They stared at us as if we were aliens from another planet! This is truly out in the boondocks. No cyclists. Not even carts, except for a lone farmer followed by a little donkey who walked slowly up the road ahead of us. There was little evidence that only six years previously, on June 6, 1944, the D-Day Invasion took place less than 200 kilometers from these steep mountains.

"We were *never* lost," Hank insisted when we stopped for a much needed rest. "Maybe I've been slightly disoriented, but one is lost only when he has to ask for help."

"But if neither of us knows where we are, how can *I* be lost when *you* aren't? Why didn't you ask that farmer for directions? Probably has something to do with your male ego."

"If we hadn't taken these narrow roads through the woods, we would never have seen all those amazing water pumps," he replied.

"Water pumps? You mean we have come all this way to see water pumps along this back road?" But I had to admit that one pump with a chain-driven handle was quite different. Yes, quite different. A brass chain, a bit larger than a bicycle chain, manipulated the lever connected to the piston in the cylinder. This seemed to force air upward, creating a vacuum. At first, icy cold water trickled out, then it came in great gushes. Only a left-handed person would appreciate how another pump worked. It only pumped water if the handle was cranked counterclockwise. While I washed my hands, a spotted cow waited patiently for a drink. Small signs along the road indicated that well water was not purified and should only be used for watering livestock along the road.

I followed Hank on this road less traveled, and hoped to live long enough to tell about the difference it had made in my life.

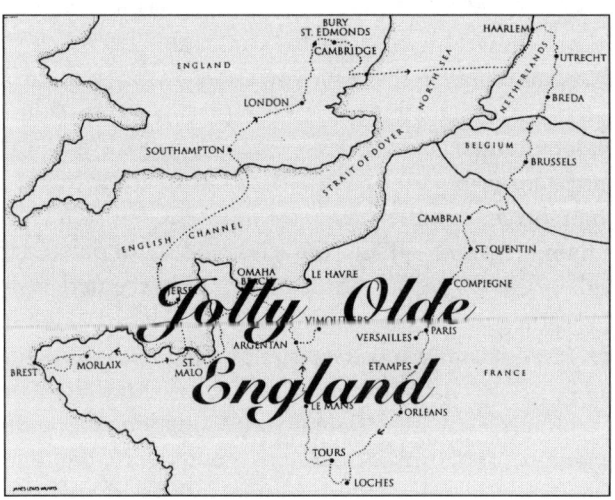

*J*t was a very long day before we returned to Morlaix. During dinner at the Grande Terrase, we had our first taste of genuine Alsatian kirsch, a dry colorless brandy distilled from fermented juice of black morello cherries. Down the narrow cobbled street in front of the sidewalk cafe was a fifteenth-century église and a viaduct built to carry the east-west rail line above the narrowing estuary. Brittany juts into the Atlantic, giving it a long heritage with the sea, but rails now linked the region with the wider world to the east. We would leave the next day for England, and I looked forward to further fascinating adventures.

We boarded the train at 11:15 and arrived at St. Brieuc before noon. The train would take us to Dinard where we would cross the inlet to St. Malo then board the ferry for England. We had a picnic of strange soft reddish cheese, bread and bitter cider in a small public park and made plans for the night. Hank worried because he did not have a map of England or London to study along the way.

Our bicycles were hung from ceiling hooks in an open freight car, and we boarded a rather antique passenger car with freshly-painted straight wooden seats and wide open windows. Throughout most of France, unforgettable lonely wails of the proud old "Lord of the Iron Road" have been overtaken by fast autorails and diesel engines. But not here in St. Brieuc. The plump little steam locomotive rocked along even though it had been heavily damaged by American aircraft during the invasion. The engine gave a few nervous puffs and sighs, then growled and spewed dense clouds of vapor and pungent black smoke from its coal-burning firebox, building up steam for the long journey ahead. It wasn't long before I began to wonder if we would make it at all.

The engine chugged merrily over several mountainous slopes until we were a few miles past Plancoet. Then in the dark of night, I heard a loud hiss of steam and slow groans followed by a loud belching sound. The train stopped and we began to roll slowly back down the incline. For a few moments, only the cold night wind broke the deathly silence, then the little engine gave a big sigh, hissed again, and black soot came streaming through the cracks in the windows. There was another loud groan and we began creeping slowly forward. I held my breath. Would we make it? The wheels gave a loud crunching sound and began to roll. I could feel the little engine puff up and say, "I *think* I can. I *think* I can." A few more hisses and it chugged forward very slowly. "I *know* I can! I *know* I can. . . ." There was another endless wait—shovels clattered as coal was hurriedly thrown into the little engine. Finally there was a loud blast of steam and we pulled over the last steep hill, shown on Hank's map as an incline of << 7% >>, we then coasted into Dinard at about midnight. Only one hotel was open—for a whopping 880 francs! It had been a very long night.

The vedette we boarded the next morning, on June 7, swirled and gyrated restlessly across the inlet to St. Malo. We were scheduled to board the SS *Isle of Jersey* before the tide ebbed. Hee-Haw and Hadacol were quickly stored in the hold of the ferry along with crates of freight neatly placed between a row of automobiles and an assortment of racing bikes to keep them company. They looked rather lonesome alongside glistening ten-speeds with flashy helmets locked to handlebars. It is remarkable how dark and musty a ferry looks—and smells—down in the hold where cargo of every description is placed. From the outside, big passenger liners seem so proud, with rhyme and reason all their own, going their own way on their own voyages. They seem to have a true relationship with the sea. But a ferry is different. It is assigned a single duty and does it without fanfare, making frequent stops, and keeping its schedule almost to the second. The ferry we were on traveled during the day, so we hoped to have one last glimpse of Mont Saint Michel to the southeast before passing several tiny islands that dot the Channel.

The French call the Channel "La Manche," meaning the sleeve of the arm which separates France from England. We stayed inside the lounge as strong winds swept across the deck. About 350 miles long, the Channel is often rough sailing when currents from the North Sea and the Atlantic meet in water that is sometimes 300 feet deep. Our crossing was quite smooth, however, despite the wind, and we arrived at St. Helier on the Isle of Jersey about noon. As expected, a small herd of contented Jersey cows slowly chewed their cuds and stared at us with sad brown eyes. The Isles of Jersey and Guernsey are perhaps best known for their dairy breeds, but far back in history they were part of England's once great Dukedom of Normandy. Cattle from the islands are familiar to folks in South Texas. The creamery in Brooks County is famous for its sweet cream butter from Jersey cows. Even the high school football team was named for them. Near Corpus Christi, Hank's father worked with a dairyman who had imported a number of Jerseys from the isle just before Hitler invaded Poland in 1939.

Most of the people on Jersey spoke stilted English, French being the official language although the islands remain part of the United Kingdom. Everyone was helpful, in a very British sort of way, but we had to push our bicycles through winding streets for two hours before finding an affordable place for the night. Unlike Normandy and Brittany where we saw few tourists, it was High Season on Jersey and hotels were not particularly interested in "one night" guests. The isle was our first experiment with the "bed and breakfast" system, which we found more expensive than hotels in France. Here, a B&B included breakfast of porridge, ham, eggs, broiled tomatoes, and, of course all the hot tea or coffee we could drink. We were both quite hungry and ate eagerly while chatting with a young Swiss fellow sitting alone at the next table. He became especially interested when Hank told him of our plans to attend the University of Fribourg. The young man then pushed his plate aside and, shrugging his shoulders, admitted the food here was decent enough, but not nearly as delicious as we would get in Switzerland. An elderly gentleman in an expensive tweed jacket and cap sat near a window table. In very proper staccato-English, he twice asked the waiter to repeat something, then turning to us, he mumbled something about the "awful brogue of the Jersians."

The channel was pocked with many reefs and small rocky islands near the Isle of Sark. It was a busy tourist port, as was Guernsey where we made another quick stop. In Southampton, the fabled passenger liner Queen Elizabeth was at the pier. A tiny English woman with tears in her eyes turned to Hank and asked, "Isn't she beautiful?" Indeed she was.

Deckhands on the ferry, in denim pants and wool caps quickly tossed mooring lines on the pier and passengers began moving about anxiously. I was eager to join them until a seaman announced that we had to retrieve our bicycles down in the hold. A fat man with a bushy red beard groaned as he mounted his bicycle and slowly churned his way up the ramp and disappeared in the early-morning fog. It was then I realized that the hold of a ferry is one of the few places my bicycle and I could not wiggle out ahead of cars or other passengers. A man in a dark uniform told me I could not push my bicycle up the ramp to the deck, but would have to pedal. In high gear, my front wheel kept slipping through great chasms in the ramp and I was almost overcome with fumes and sputters of waiting automobiles. A few speedy cyclists charged quickly ahead. Hank disappeared through a narrow opening between a row of cyclists. I tried to follow close behind when suddenly my bicycle hit a wide gap in the ramp. I heard a loud thud and saw nuts and bolts fly from the rear wheel. Everyone seemed to have disappeared as I looked helplessly at the chain lying limp on water-soaked planks. There is nothing more frightening than to be all alone in a jungle of exhaust fumes and anxious motorists and above all, other cyclists! Before I could call "HEEE-HAAW," the fellow from Switzerland stopped and fixed my bike on the spot while horns honked and cyclists and pedestrians applauded.

When I was actually aware of Great Britain for the first time, I was at a desk in Miss Fowler's fourth grade geography class. We had studied the United States–searching through old Progressive Farmer *magazines for pictures of wheat and grain to paste on square boxy states*

*like Colorado and Wyoming. It was quite boring for a ten-year-old who
was more familiar with watermelons and cotton gins than Colorado wheat
fields. Besides, I had rather be outside shooting marbles. But when Miss
Fowler gently laid out the map for England, Wales and Scotland, I was
all eyes! It looked like a side of beef in shades of green and pink with
squiggly veins of blue in every direction.*

This time, on June 8, England was not just a drawing on a wall
map or pictures from *National Geographic*. Even Hank's maps
seemed to come alive as he traced our route. Misty rain began to fall
in typical English fashion and the sky turned gray. Cycling through
the center of Southampton was easy enough but the benediction that
seemed to doom our search for the proper route out of the city was
the well-intended phrase: "You cawn't miss it." But we did. Several
times. It took more than an hour to cycle over surprisingly steep hills
to the small village of Chandler Ford five miles away. We found the
people a bit cold and reserved, especially at the B&B cottage.
However, on our first morning, the owner knocked at the door and
brought us a pot of hot tea and sweet pastries. B&B? A wonderful way
to wake up.

The countryside was similar to the small French villages,
though we saw fewer farmers working in the fields. Strains of war
were very evident and people still had to contend with rationing. At
a small sweet shop nestled between a bookstore and a tobacco shop
in Winchester, I picked up a bar of dark Cadbury chocolate.
Thoughts of cream and rum flavored raisins made my mouth water!

"How much?" I asked, holding out a shilling or two.

"Your coupon first, please," the clerk said. He saw my blank
expression. "AAAhh, you have not picked up your ration coupons
from the Royal Food office yet? Do that as soon as possible. Take the
chocolate anyway. Cadbury chocolate is England's very finest.
Besides, the war is over. For us, as well as you Americans."

Hank spent half an hour at the bookstore next door, trying to
find a proper map. Finally, for about thirty cents, he bought an
Ordnance Survey map printed in dull colors but showing topogra-
phy and a variety of other interesting facts and numerous less-
traveled routes we might take. We soon learned that England has a
few inclines and descents of its own, but they were not marked on
the map with "<<" and ">>" as in France. As the highways became

steeper and the hills more numerous, we decided not to go towards Stratford-upon-Avon in Warwickshire but cycle directly to London. We passed Blackwater, then found a nice B&B in a Victorian-style house at Camberley. Before dinner, we walked through a deep pine forest near Sandhurst, best known as the "West Point of England," where Winston Churchill received his military training. Hedges of beautiful rhododendrons—pink, blue and white—bordered the campus of the Royal Military College.

We left in mid-morning, arriving on the southwestern outskirts of London before noon. Wide streets were lined with slate gray buildings that seemed to be held together by rows of chimneys and topped with delicate wiry television antennas. We were amazed, because TV sets were not yet available for the average American, or at least not in South Texas. We turned off at a small place called "The

Cannon at Sandhurst, the "West Point of England."

Woods" and went a short distance up a gravel road to what looked like a public park. Hank spread his field jacket on the grass as the sun broke through the clouds and it got hot and humid. A winding driveway bordered by rhododendrons led to an imposing gray museum-like building covered with ivy, where we hoped to get a glass of cool water. No one answered when Hank knocked at the heavily carved door. We went around to the back area. PRIVATE, the sign said. Hank knocked again. A very tall woman in a white apron opened the door slowly and looked down at me through thick rimmed glasses. She studied Hank's worn clothing and the wicker basket tied to my bicycle, then put her hands on her hips and gave me a questioning look.

"Trespassing? Oh, no ma'am. There was a sign on the gate that said this was The Woods. We thought it was a public park!" I said innocently. "It's a private residence?"

She pushed her glasses up on her sharp nose, and replied stiltedly, "This is the residence of Lord ——. It is *not* a public park." Then she shook her head and added, "Despite a bit of damage during the War, the Woods will never *ever* be taken over and made into a museum by the National Trust like many proud homes in

Last rest on the outskirts of London.

London." She waved her arms towards the vast wooded area and repeated, "Its history goes back hundreds of years and I can assure you it is even more valuable today!"

We got the message. Loud and clear. Surely we were not the first strangers to mistake the lovely private residence for a public park.

"Please wait," she said sharply and returned with a tray, a pitcher of cool water and two crystal glasses.

We had much to learn about England.

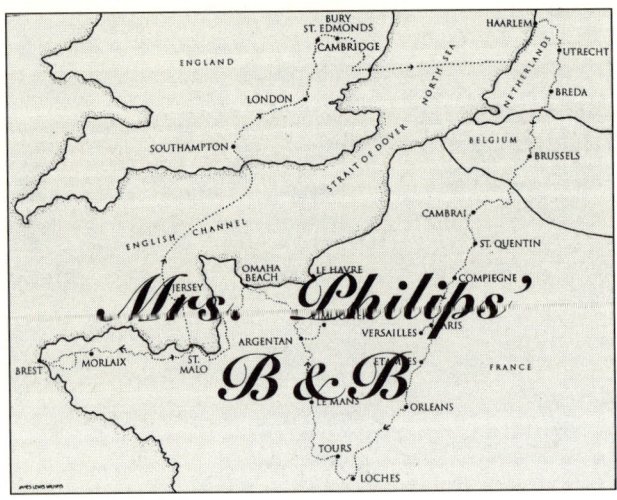

The blitz in London had caused damages far greater than any we saw in France, except maybe in the port area of Le Havre and the tiny village of Vimoutiers. The traffic was wild and reckless and I longed for the quietness of the French countryside. Blitz bombs left a great many streets in the world's largest city covered with ruins or pocked by craters, although the Reconstruction Minister was moving fast to have them rebuilt. How strange it was to roll along wide avenues dodging potholes as well as cars, taxis, buses, vans and a few horse-drawn wagons. A huge cart horse—broad-beamed and stately, with feathered hocks and a glittering brass-trimmed harness—came lumbering up behind me then passed, weaving in and out among the traffic. Imagine having a ribbon braided in the tail of a horse that size! It could happen only in London.

The noise of construction crews was deafening, but it was more difficult adjusting to the rumble of traffic, even though it was the "light" traffic of a Saturday afternoon. I looked neither right nor left as boxy taxicabs made U-turns in the middle of the street. Stiff-collared men with mousy mustaches, black suits and bowlers carried leather briefcases in and out of the Bank of England.

At one wide intersection, Hank slowed a bit then suddenly shoved off before the light changed to red. A bobby in a blue uniform and helmet stood in the center of the street. I was expecting to catch up with Hank, until I heard a shrill whistle and saw the bobby's gloved hand go up, stopping me cold. Automobiles continued to flash by, left-to-right. I wrapped my hands frantically around the brake lever and slid from the seat—hard—my feet anchored on the asphalt. People hurried in all directions. A monstrous red double-deck bus, groaning and hissing, stopped inches behind me. Its folding door flew open and several passengers emerged. There was a hissing noise like an old man passing gas, and the grating sound of gears shifting. I had never given much thought to the wheezes and grunts of city buses because never before had I been approached so intimately by one. It was most frightening to see Hank whirring away down the street.

"HEEE-HAAW!" I wailed. "Wait for me, H-A-A-A-N-K! Wait. . . ." The policeman turned sharply, giving me a strange look, as did the pedestrians on the sidewalk. The light finally turned green and traffic began to move. I heard Hank's echo "HAD-A-C-O-L!" and knew he would never abandon me—besides, I had our passport in my purse! Gears shifted again, the bus gave a grunt or two and everything was caught in a cloud of thick exhaust fumes. To my amazement, the bobby held up his billy stick and all traffic stopped again— buses, taxis, automobiles and trucks; men with black umbrellas and women pushing strollers. An old street sweeper in a long shaggy coat rested his straw broom as he waited to see what was happening. With a sweeping motion, the bobby motioned me forward, but I was too shaken. After another deathly silence, a few automobiles beeped and a jolly old woman gave my bicycle a slight shove, saying with a distinct brogue, "Your go, Sweetie."

The bobby bowed formally and his gloved hand made a sweeping motion. I shoved off, double quick. "HEEE-HAAW, I'm coming . . . !" People began to shuffle off as if nothing happened.

A small B&B sign hung over a doorway at 186 Gower Street. Dark and musty, the place looked as if it had been through trying times. However, it was clean and inexpensive. Nearby were Euston Square and the Tube Station of the underground railway, winding

Telephone. EUSton

MRS. ROBINSON.
Bed and Breakfast.
THE COTTAGE,
6, MELTON STREET,
LONDON, N.W.1.

Opposite Euston Station. Near King's
Cross and St. Pancras Station.

3 minutes West End.

Mrs. Philips' B&B: "We survived the Blitz!"

under London's streets like the Metro of Paris. Mrs. Philips, the landlady, answered the tinkling doorbell, and greeted us like old friends. A fat grandmotherly sort, she talked constantly as she huffed her way upstairs to our room.

"You from Texas? Wonderful! Leave your bags, lock your bicycles then come join us in the basement for tea," she said. "I've just served some of my special marzipan cakes to my friend, Mrs. Robinson. We are planning a trip to Oklahoma soon. Do you know where that is? I read that it's out west where the Indians are," she said excitedly.

"We do hope to see real cowboys in ten-gallon hats and boots," Mrs. Robinson said, after we were properly introduced. She leaned over to hand Hank her business card. "Aye, I also have a B&B—'The Cottage' at 6 Melton Street, only three minutes from the West End. Some say that's only where wealthy people spend money, make laws and create fashions," she chuckled proudly, "but ne'er you mind. I'm just a 'Coc' like Mrs. Philips—and that's all I want to be."

The women then began chattering in their sharp cockney accents, interrupting each other with yarns about the blitz and V-bomb days. The war was still very much with them.

Years later, I thought about these two women when I heard Simon and Garfunkel sing "Here's to you, Mrs. Robinson. Sitting on a sofa on a Sunday afternoon. Laugh about it, shout about it. Hey. Hey. Hey."

"During the war, hundreds of Londoners were left homeless," Mrs. Philips said, beginning another story about the devastation they had endured. "After the war, at least ten thousand of the Royal Army's small Nissen huts were used as emergency shelters."

"Ah, yes my dear, but remember that was only a fraction of the homes that were destroyed," Mrs. Robinson interrupted, leaning over to pour herself another cup of tea. "You should have seen our blackout curtains. After five years, we raised them cautiously for the first time. Was it '44 or '45? Ne'er mind. We hung them back quickly because as long as bombs were fallin' we decided it would be wise to keep sensibly dark. Remember the doodlebugs, Mrs. Philips?"

"Ah, indeed I do. Well, it was early one morning. . ." Mrs. Philips began, sitting back in her soft chair. Mrs. Robinson chuckled, having heard the story many times before. "Yes, quite early it was when the doodlebugs—V-bombs or rockets or whatever—came rumbling over the city. I decided, 'itler or no 'itler, I was going to fry meself a precious egg. I broke it in the skillet then the first doodlebug came over. So, I turned off the stove and ran for shelter. This happened eight times, mind you. By then, me precious egg was a dull blue and gray color in the center and a dark brown around the edges." She threw back her head and laughed so hard her face turned red.

"She swore she would not let her precious egg spoil for no 'itler! She could 'ave put a pin through it and wore it for a broach, she could 'ave," Mrs. Robinson said, removing her thick glasses to wipe tears of laughter away.

"Cor—you are such a twit!" Mrs. Philips replied, covering her face with her apron in embarrassment.

"Buzz bombs were the worst," Mrs. Robinson continued. "Believe it was about a week after the Invasion. Yes, only a week or so after Mr. 'itler sent buzz bombs bursting all over London. Total chaos! *The Times* called them 'vengeance weapons,' or V-1's, but the Germans called them *'wergeltungswaffles'* or something like that."

"Vergeltung-*swaffes*, my dear. *Swaffes*, not waffles! You folks from America surely don't want to hear anymore war stories," Mrs. Philips said, slicing another thick piece of marzipan.

Hank moved to the table to study his blue covered map of London, but Mrs. Philips quickly began a tale of her own about their trip to the mountains in the Lake Country.

"We had a fine map, very fine indeed, and we followed it ever so closely. As I drove merrily down the motorway, I noticed my friend here bending low, tracing the little red lines on the map with her finger. 'Are we 'bout there?' I asked. You know what she said? She said, 'Bout *there*? No, dearie, I am praying to St. Anthony that we are going in the right direction!'"

The humor of the women was evident in their chatter, even though they still had vivid memories of the war years. "Ah . . . my dears. We were more fortunate than those along the coast. 'Bomb Alley,' we call it," Mrs. Philips said with a faraway look in her eyes. "Actually sometimes I rather miss it." She poured Hank another cup of tea and watched as he emptied his pockets of coins, separating nickels and francs from a few pence and shillings. "Here, we call it tuppence and thruppence," she said. "Now, one British pound is roughly four American dollars; a shilling, twenty cents; sixpence a dime. See? Half crown, two shillings and sixpence—2s, 6d or 2/6. Actually, it's quite simple."

We retired early and woke to a dreary sky the next morning, June 10. "Aye. Rain again," Mrs. Philips said, handing Hank a damp morning tabloid. "British weather, like British courtesy, has sagged badly during the years, and I'm afraid neither has recovered," she moaned, shaking her head.

"Oh, I wouldn't say that, Mrs. Philips," I said. "You and Mrs. Robinson are examples of the wonderful people we've met. Not only that, you also make the most delicious marzipan cakes I've ever tasted! (I didn't tell her I'd never tasted it before.) Everyone—the policemen, the clerks at the sweets shop and bookstore—has been so very helpful. And thank goodness, no more fractured French!"

"You're so sweet," she said as she placed our breakfast on the table. And what a breakfast—kipper and country sausage, broiled tomatoes, bittersweet marmalade, old-fashioned Scots porridge, toast and coffee.

"No grits?" Hank asked, putting the paper aside.

"Grits?" Mrs. Philips gave him a blank look then laughed. "Ah— you Texans do tease!" She pulled a chair to the table and began to chatter again. "Now you take carrots. Cook 'em cleverly and serve 'em nice, I always say. It's lucky for us Lord Woolton always had his supply of corn beef to help us out during the War. Ah, those were the days. Cold or hot, I could dish it up in a dozen different ways . . .

very tasty, too." She pulled the lace curtains back and looked at the dark rain-soaked sky. "'Tis another soft day. But don't you worry, spring showers are a fine old British institution."

"Wasn't it Ralph Waldo Emerson who said good rain is like a bad preacher—because it doesn't know when to leave off," Hank teased. "We always look forward to rainy spells in Texas." We could hear Mrs. Philips chuckling in the kitchen. Hank turned again to the gray tabloid and buried his head in headlines, something about the firm hand of socialist Britain on state directed mines, communication failures, railway strikes, and the ever demanding assists needed in agriculture, housing, education and the National Health Service.

"Look at that advertisement!" I said, pointing to a story on the back page: "WANTED—an Egyptian or semi-Egyptian Donkey—not a female—to take an old lady for drives in a wheelchair."

"That must mean Great Britain is getting back to good living," Hank said, turning to Mrs. Philips. "Now that the government freed gasoline from tight rationing and loosened other restrictions, haven't most people begun to feel that the era of prewar abundance and freedom is close at hand?"

"I hope 'tis true," she replied. "However, I caution you to be aware of shysters. They're still around, even though blackmarketeers are finding it quite difficult to buy up coupons to sell at double the price. You will see canned fish, rice, syrup and cookies now available at the markets. And shoes. It's been a very long time." She looked down at her heavy black oxfords then at my brown loafers and Hank's size 12s. "Do take care, dearie. Surely you're not going out in this rain. And you have no umbrella? No need to worry, dearie. It won't last long."

Mrs. Philips helped me put on my red sweater. "Ah, a quotation from Shelley!" she said in amazement, "never saw poetry on a coat!" She warned Hank about the traffic going left to right, and hurried us out as the sun slowly broke through the drizzle. Our first morning was a continuous damp blur as we strolled down one winding street after the other until I thought we would walk forever. Then the sun began to shine, giving a sudden fresh smell of spring just as the English poet had said. Of all the unusual things I saw that day, I believe the most shocking were the tiny words, "Government Property" printed on every single sheet of toilet paper in Public Toilets, called "the loo." I must admit I took one home to show mother.

Orators stood on soap boxes arguing over world affairs. If England would accept more socialism things would be better, one proclaimed to a small crowd. A short distance away, others were blaming the United States, the Labor government or the Church of England for the good, bad or indifferent world crisis. Laborites blamed Conservatives, and vice versa. In a circus-like atmosphere, they seemed to be celebrating their great freedom of speech. It was Londoners' way of gradually settling down to a peacetime routine as they tried desperately to patch their wounds from the blitz, doodle-bugs and buzz bombs.

"Actually, England doesn't seem quite so different from America," Hank commented as we stopped at a small sidewalk cafe for tea and biscuits. "Meals have more variety now that the five shilling (seventy cents) limit on restaurant charges has been lifted. According to the paper, removing government restrictions also brought with it an end to a great deal of bureaucratic red tape and paper work."

"But that probably means many jobs have been eliminated because of it," I added. "I'm sure grocers and ministry clerks aren't complaining. Just imagine having to cut and count millions of coupons like they did for so many years."

After lunch, we walked towards St. James's Park off Trafalgar Square and Hank bought a small bouquet of spring flowers from a little gray-haired lady pushing a heavy cart. Swans and geese strutted through the dankish grass, and formal hedges in full bloom added to the colorful atmosphere. The statue of Peter Pan across Kensington Gardens had been worn smooth by childrens' loving caresses.

Sheep grazed alongside young artists, who were bending low on the sidewalk and drawing gaudy chalk scenes and modernistic designs that would quickly disappear in the night mist. Their "art" is beautiful compared to the graffiti that defaces the city of Dallas. Elderly women sat on park benches and talked softly as they fed crumbs of bread to cooing pigeons. Across the way, small boys played soccer, wearing identical school uniforms of short navy blue pants and white shirt tails sticking out in all sorts of disarray. A group of teenagers scuffled and a young couple whispered sweet nothings under a small shrub.

After tea, we walked around the House of Parliament and down the dead-end street to an unimpressive gray building, No. 10 Downing Street, the official residence of Britain's prime minister. The weather began to get quite warm and sultry between frequent showers, but at Buckingham Palace guards continued to wear above-the-knee black boots, white spotless leather pants, bright red jackets, gloves and "bushies." Bright red plumes denoted cadets, blue plumes officers. Sentries marched with drawn swords. Very British!

At the entrance to the Tube, passengers were cautioned not to move in the Underground "whilst in motion." City maps showed Tube lines crisscrossing each other like patterns of fancy embroidery. Hank insisted they were not real maps at all because they were not drawn to scale. We quickly found this out when, in some cases, we could have walked the same distance in a few minutes. At Soho near Charing Cross was a network of crooked, narrow streets where foreigners had contributed to an elusive atmosphere and distinct flavor. We stopped at a cluster of booksellers, which unlike stores in America, had soft chairs where browsers could sit undisturbed and read all afternoon. I had a difficult time prying Hank away after he found a copy of Sean O'Faolain's new book about the art of writing. It had been reviewed recently in the overseas edition of *Time*. Something else to carry around, I thought as he stuffed it in his pocket with his maps. Exotic aromas drew me towards tiny restaurants— Egyptian, Italian, French, Turkish, Swiss, Chinese, Indian, Jewish, Danish.

The next morning, we found ourselves unexpectedly on London's famous Fleet Street. Journalism professors at the university had lectured about the great newspapers of the world, and especially the wonders of this fabled street. *The Times* was suddenly real, not simply narrow columns on gray pages found in an awesome library. Hank found another map of London and Great Britain at a dignified newsstand near the Times building. The twin Foldex had a scale of one inch to ten miles; easy enough to read, but impossible to refold. The clerk blamed the high price of 7/6 (about $1.50) on recent paper rationing. In the middle of the block, a sturdy wall was being constructed around a deep ugly crater, all that was left of St. Brides Church. A sign placed nearby read: "Flyposters will be prosecuted." The church was being rebuilt for the eighth time in its history. This time, workers finally had uncovered the ruins of the first church, built at a time when Christians had to stay outside of the nearby wall encircling Roman Londonum.

Throughout the day, we walked the streets or went in and out of the Underground from one great place to another. To actually walk along the River Thames was to travel back twelve or more centuries when it was a means of transportation for kings in their royal barges rather than an inexpensive way for Londoners to escape the city's noise and turmoil. Hank added this note to be used in his weekly newspaper articles back home.

It cost 6d to enter the iron gates of the Tower of London. Cold stone floors reeked of history, as did the tiny rooms hidden behind thick walls. One guide in a traditional Beefeater uniform told us we were standing exactly where Ann Boleyn walked across the Tower Green "with 'er 'ead tucked beneath 'er arms." The Tower was begun by William the Conqueror, first to protect the city, then to gain control. We walked on the same cobblestones that first led to a fortress, then a palace, a prison, the Royal Mint, and for a short time, the Royal Observatory. Then we crossed a moat, now dry, where once there had been a drawbridge. In 1928, a severe storm swept a tidal wave over the wharf, destroying portions of the moat's retaining walls and flooding the Byward Tower to a depth of four feet.

Beefeaters have lived at the Tower since the seventeenth century. Their original duty was to taste the King's food to protect him from being poisoned. Also living in the thriving Tower community are soldiers whose primary duty is to protect the crown jewels. A Ravenmaster had clipped the wings of the ravens to keep them from flying away. "It is believed that bad things happen if ever there are no ravens at the Tower," he explained. Despite romantic tales of prisoners drowning at high tide, the dungeon is more than ten feet above the highest water mark. Even though the Tower was not built as a prison, a total of over 1,700 prisoners have been hurled into the basement or locked in the Tower. World War II created its own share of history when the bastion was destroyed by a German bomb in 1940. It has not been rebuilt. The most recent execution held there was in 1941 when a German spy was shot by a firing squad. The German sergeant parachuted into England, was injured in landing, and captured quickly. A far more important member of Hitler's Germany, Rudolf Hess, was held briefly at the Tower after the German leader flew to Scotland in a Messerschmitt BF110. There was some thought that he was trying to bring about an end to the war. In any case, he was held at the Tower for four days before a long imprisonment and eventual return to Germany for the famed War Trials following V-E Day.

We roamed around until the hazy sun dropped behind the Tower walls and suddenly it was time to leave. On the way back along the tree-shaded river, we stopped at a tea garden. A waiter pointed out what he claimed was the site of Shakespeare's old dressing room, now used as part of a pub. He also told us that Winchester Wharf occupies the site of the lovely Old Globe Theatre. London has survived many disasters: the terrible plague of 1665 followed the next year by the Great Fire, the zeppelin raids of German airships during World War I and more recently the great blitz.

As much as I enjoyed hearing the stories and seeing the places, I knew these historic events were more meaningful to Hank than to me. He relished the historical London where such authors and poets as Keats, Dickens, and Thackeray lived. His guide books and his maps were vital to his enjoyment. My interest in London was mostly curiosity. I liked the exotic smells, the soft colors. I didn't need maps.

I wanted to linger in battered St. Paul's Cathedral that had stood firm through some of the worst destruction in London during WWII. That bombing resulted in one of the most beautiful views of the majestic cathedral, one Londoners had not seen for many many years. When first completed in 1710, the view must have been magnificent. However, through the years, it became surrounded by tall buildings, wide streets, noisy taxis and racing automobiles. This was suddemly changed when a German buzz bomb cleared the area and the Cathedral was again visible for all the world to see! The cathedral is Sir Christopher Wren's greatest contribution to the rebuilding of the city following the Great Fire of 1666.

We could not visit the Natural History Museum in the western part of the city or Madame Tussaud's famed wax work museum, for they had been damaged. Repairs were underway. I noticed that life in many areas had settled down to a peacetime routine with the traditional British reserve. A few barrow boys still sold fruit and vegetables, but the muffin men, whelk men, rabbitskin men and the cat's meat boys had disappeared from the streets. A young boy pushing his barrow of fruit and vegetables stopped singing as we bought a few oranges from his cart. He was dressed in knickers and a wool cap, just like one of Dicken's characters. He quickly bragged that he was one of the "vanishing scenes" of London. The whelk men with their carts of snails and muffin men with warm buns were now only in rural areas. The young boy reminded me of the old blind Mexican man back home who, with his grandson leading him, brought hot tamales to town every Friday afternoon. Delicious! However, the city still enjoyed what was perhaps the most dignified and courtly group of doormen in the world.

According to Hank, it would be "only a few blocks farther" to Westminster Abbey—but very long winding blocks—where much of England's great history had taken place. The floor plan of the Gothic structure is in the traditional shape of a Latin Cross and a plaque notes that almost all of England's rulers from the time of William the Conqueror have been crowned there. These kings and queens are buried beneath the worn stone floor. The familiar names of some of the world's greatest poets are carved in Poet's Corner. In one small nave, a simple grave is dedicated to the Unknown Warrior of the 1914–18 war. Air raids during the Second World War shattered walls and damaged many stained glass windows. One was being replaced by a beautiful memorial to the Royal Air Force.

While riding on the Tube late on our last afternoon in London, I told Hank about the fellow back home who married an English girl whose mother owned the Lichester Hotel near Euston Station. Lou was quite different, naturally, from girls who grew up in our ranching country. Her hair was bleached a shocking platinum color and had a touch of bluish rinse on top. She had met Bob, a young lieutenant stationed at an American air base near London who, like most airmen, looked quite sharp in his Air Corps uniform or leather flight jacket. A few weeks after he returned home when the war was over, Lou arrived unexpectedly at the bus station at Casey's Cafe. She was looking for Bob. Some people thought it was the most exciting thing to happen since a truckload of watermelons overturned on Main Street.

Bob had no intentions of marrying her, but Lou stayed around town, flirting with other boys home from the service. She eventually met Johnny, an army sergeant who had been wounded in the Pacific. I remember visiting him at an army hospital in California before I was discharged from the Navy. Before long, Lou and Johnny were flying off to London to be married. In Westminster Abbey, no less! Needless to say, they created plenty of small town gossip! Why would a flighty young British girl want to marry someone from dusty South Texas? I was just finishing the story when we crossed the busy street and went up narrow stairs to the small Lichester desk where we had hoped to say hello to Lou's mother—but we were told Lou's mother was "on holiday."

Mrs. Philips had tea waiting for us on our return. After Hank told her of the historical places we had visited, I listed the wonderful food we had eaten. I couldn't seem to get enough fish and chips, neatly wrapped in newspaper and selling for 2/6 from vendors with two-wheeled carts. During the week, we had lunch in smoke-filled pubs with dart boards and weak draught stout. Tables were small and round and the barmaids called Hank "Honey." He didn't seem to mind. Each day's menu was displayed on a small blackboard at the front of the pubs: Rabbit Pie, 6d; Braised Liver, 6d (with vegetables) and Sultans roll, 2d; Rice Pudding, 2d and Lentil Soup, 1d, and something called Potato Foddies. I didn't tell Mrs. Philips that I thought most vegetables in London seemed to be treated as enemies and chastened by overboiling.

"It seems many kinds of foods have gradually become more plentiful, but you continue to accept Lord Woolton's food rationing," I said.

"Oh dearie me, Lord Woolton does indeed take care of us," Mrs. Philips replied. "My grocer still keeps a small faded sign in front of his store that says: 'Those who have the will to win will cook potatoes in their skin, knowing that the right of peeling, deeply hurts Lord Woolton's feelings.'"

Hank studied his maps while Mrs. Philips began telling him of the strange names of some of England's tongue-titillating villages. "You will find places like Great Snoring and Little Snoring, Piddletrenthide, Pye Corner Gwent, Nasty, Crackpot, and Ugley," she said.

"Here's a place I can't pronounce. Have you ever heard of Pwillmeyric?" I added, pointing to a tiny speck on his map. "I notice that some have earthy tones and descriptive character like Newbiggin-by-the-Sea and Waltham on the Wald. The tiny village of Cat's Bottom is down near the Wash. I remember a little place in Normandy, west of Caen, I think, named Rots. We spent the night there. And near Mortree was a hamlet named O. Nothing more."

"Oh? What do you mean, oh? Oh what?" she asked.

"Oh nothing. Just O."

"O? OOOoooo! You Americans do tease! No? Ahhhh, you'd better go to bed, dearie. You've had a hard day. . . ."

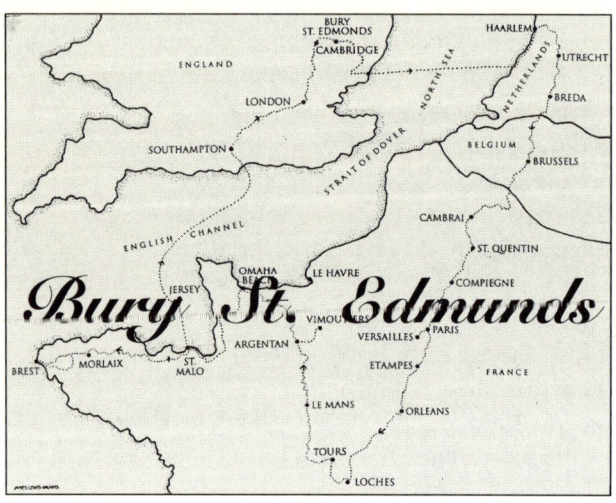

$\mathcal{I}$ was a dreary morning–June 13 —when we loaded our bicycles to leave after almost a week in London. The weather was chilly and clouds sagged and turned leaden color. It didn't begin to rain until we reached the outskirts of the city near lunchtime. Across rolling hills were concrete pillboxes built to protect London in case of German invasions. Later we passed several abandoned aircraft runways, bringing back memories of the great exploits of the Royal Air Force. Along the highway were bolted steel Quonsets, now used as barns instead of military barracks. Huts were also provided to ease the housing shortage in Surrey County where 1,425 families were left homeless. Unfortunately, the council's program allotted only 135 structures. Unlike France, where villages were frantically rebuilding homes, England was constructing more council halls and government buildings, leaving families on a long waiting list to get permission to rebuild.

We cycled towards Saffron Walden about forty miles north of London hoping to find an inexpensive B&B. From there, we proceeded a few miles off the highway to the village of Hixton and

122

had tea in the home of Mary Howe. She was a teenager who participated last year in a 4-H Exchange Program in the Corpus Christi area where Hank's father served as county agent for the Texas Agricultural Extension Service.

The Howes' home was modest and inviting, and I was most impressed by the highly polished copper pots and pans hanging from ceiling hooks over a large work table in the center of the kitchen. Mary was very knowledgeable about the declining farm situation in England and anxious to show us their farm. Under Atlee's socialistic government, she said, sixty percent of the farmers rent their land. The dramatic need for food during the war led to more intensive scientific farming, and if the land was not used to its fullest advantage, a government committee had the power to take it back. Farm labor in England is unionized, a fact the farmers apparently never forget.

She introduced us to Mr. Webster, a "gentleman farmer" who, with his two sons, had been renting a 360-acre farm for over thirty years from St. John's College of Cambridge University. They followed an intensive program, raising cereal grain crops and operating a certified dairy as well as raising broilers. Mr. Webster served on the Agricultural Council which graded every farm annually for efficiency level. If no improvements were shown, the Council could begin legal proceedings.

"But a farmer seldom actually loses his farm," Mr. Webster explained. "Several years might pass before action is taken."

After we returned to Saffron, Hank noted in his journal that farmers in "Olde England" seem to have lost their right to own property. His home is no longer his castle!

It was quite late before we returned to our B&B along a rolling gravel road. It was a beautiful night, and I enjoyed cycling under the arms of tall willowy trees until the headlight generator on my front wheel flickered, then went out. Everything suddenly changed into dark mysterious expanses of deadly silence, broken by the occasional hoot of an owl. I gave my trusty "HEEE-HAAW" plea and Hank slowed, so the dim little generator light of his bicycle led us safely back to the B&B.

Early the next morning, we cycled through several villages where church spires rose majestically into the hazy sky. Light poured down on them like a blessing from an invisible source, like in John Constable's paintings. Trees arched up, framing the spires while

Marie Alsmeyer with porter at Peterhouse, Cambridge University.

cows grazed and drank from nearby ponds. We finally reached Cambridge, one of England's most famous university cities, which circles more than twenty separate ivy covered "colleges." Most of the buildings are built of mellow stones and centered around lush green plots in ancient quadrangles. The halls and chapels, reflecting the monastic times of the Middle Ages heritage of these colleges, overflow with history, academic and otherwise. Each college has its own faculty, classrooms, chapels and dorms.

There were few automobiles. Local people have learned that the easiest way to navigate the winding streets is on bicycles. We parked ours along with hundreds of others at entryways or leaned them against buttress-like stone walls. Spring term had just ended and students loaded with books hurried across the campus with their long robes hanging loosely from their shoulders. The city of Cambridge and the colleges are closely united now, but one student told us that it hasn't always been that way. At one time, students were opposed to more streetlights because they were afraid it would increase fighting between "town and gown."

We located a lovely little B&B across from a campus near the River Cam. From a nearby bridge, surprisingly like pictures of the famous Bridge of Sighs in Venice, we could see students "punting the Cam." Young men stood at one end of a flat-bottomed boat and propelled it with long poles while young women reclined comfortably at the other end. Cambridge men claim they propel from the "wrong" end to preserve their identity.

The only connecting links between the colleges are porters wearing black suits, black shoes and black derby hats. Each of the twenty-three colleges has separate laws and customs to govern them, but they are also subject to the laws of the university. When I look back, I will always think of the Porter of Peterhouse College (Saint Peter's College). Unlike Mrs. Philips and the rattling cockney folks we met in London, this Porter spoke very correct "Oxbridge" English with a rather "brawed" accent. His basic duty was to keep tab on the 200 students in his college.

"Peterhouse is the oldest of the colleges, dating to the thirteenth century," he said proudly. His historical facts spanned centuries of events and near the end, he noted that, more recently, sheep had been brought to the quad grounds to eat the grass during the first World War, so men who had been tending the lawns could be freed for military service. He then took us into the oldest apartments, with very narrow stairways that twisted around and around like climbing to the tower of a lighthouse. The ceiling was so low I bumped my head and Hank had to almost get on his hands and knees.

Cycling the next morning was fast and quite pleasant, as we went eastwards towards Harwich and the English Channel where we planned to board a ferry to the Hook of Holland. Steepled churches and numerous pastel-colored cottages, thatched roofed and half-timbered, dotted almost every picturesque village. This was rich farming country, with some areas near sea level. Not far to the north were vast level fens made from ancient swamps reclaimed several centuries ago. Like the areas around Paris, we were again cycling on wide asphalt paths that ran alongside the highway. Even so, I sometimes forgot to move to the far left when I heard tingling bells when racers came up fast from behind. They often looked back in amazement after seeing a little lady on an ordinary bicycle carrying a wicker basket. They would wave, then give a shrill whistle before zipping past.

We stopped to rest beside an abandoned runway that was probably used by the U.S. Army Air Force's "Mighty Eighth" during the war. A decaying control tower with the metal frame of a glass watch house on top stood aloof like a red brick ghost. Farmers were cutting hay and the scent blew in gusts over a strange faded sign on

He loves me. . . . He loves me not. The fresh smell of spring.

the road that read: PROHIBITED PLACE WITHIN THE MEAN OF THE OFFICIAL SECRET ACT. I laid back on the grass, closed my eyes and listened to a symphony of birds from beyond the hedgerow. Grasshoppers flitted in and out among yellow buttercups and there was a deep rich smell of warm earth, crushed grasses and a slightly stagnant pond that drugged my sleep.

As I dozed, the field suddenly seemed to vibrate with thunderous roars of Eighth Air Force B-17s lifting off the tarmac. Near the end of the abandoned runway, I could almost see the flak bursts in the icy-blue sky above enemy targets. This airfield, like so many others throughout East Anglia, had experienced many moments of glory before the war ended. The field was now left empty and derelict. I remember thinking that maybe forty or fifty years from that day, those same airmen—no longer young—would make a military pilgrimage, a last hurrah so they could put to rest bad memories. Others would be drawn by a nostalgia for the places where they accomplished the bravest and most exciting achievements of their lives. For them, these bases could again come alive with the thundering drones of planes.

We cycled through Newmarket, the famous horse racing town, on the main road to Bury St. Edmunds, where we planned to treat ourselves to a very plush four-star hotel. The Angel was truly ancient and truly four-star. In fact, I felt we should leave our bicycles on a busy corner, for they seemed out of place in front of the massive wooden doors. A withered little man was standing at the edge of the steps. He looked as ancient as The Angel itself. With his corduroys and gardener's basket, he fit perfectly with the scene. I was surprised to see someone quite young open the door and speak to us in a twentieth-century accent. I could scarcely move for fear of startling history.

It was quite evident this was no ordinary place. It took a few minutes to become accustomed to the dark panels and dim light. The desk clerk raised his eyebrows as we registered and then motioned to a young boy to pick up my basket. Silently, we followed him single file up wide hardwood stairs. At the first landing I caught a glimpse of a few elderly men gathered around a billiard table.

"Looks like fun," I whispered to Hank. The boy gave me a cutting look, and hastily pointed to a sign: MEN ONLY. Our room was pure luxury, and I could hardly wait to get into the high antique bed covered with a beautiful down comforter. From the window we could see the remains of the great medieval abbey gates. The long narrow bathroom had huge towels warming on a wall heater. There was hot water with real soap, but no washcloth. The tub, mounted on short clawed feet, was very long and very deep. In fact, I could hardly climb out of it. Most fascinating of all was the toilet. It was like a throne on a small platform, with a large almost square wooden seat. It was flushed by a pull handle reaching up to a container of water near the ceiling.

We walked very softly the next morning into the formal dining room for breakfast. Hazy sunlight was just beginning to peep from behind heavy drapes at the floor-to-ceiling windows. An elderly gentleman sitting alone unfolded his linen napkin and propped a copy of *The Times* before him. He had no reason to tell the waiter what he wanted, so regular and recurrent was his daily life. He sprinkled a bit of brown sugar on his porridge and ate a bun with marmalade from his personalized, cut glass jam container. Nearby, a tall white-haired woman, dressed to the hilt, sat very erect. She too, slowly spread toast with butter—real butter—and a tiny bit from her antique marmalade dish.

"Do you think we're dressed properly?" I whispered to Hank, looking down at my brown skirt and ankle socks.

"Of course!" he replied, but with very little confidence, wiping his hands on his khakis. We were thankful we were at a small round table in the far corner of the room, away from the permanent residents. I quickly noticed our marmalade (made from Seville oranges by James Keiller and Son Ltd.) was in a lovely pottery container bearing the label of "Dundee." Breakfast was delicious and very expensive. Mrs. Philips' B&B was never like this.

As we left, I secretly hoped we could someday come here again. We loaded our bicycles, pumped up tires and cycled over more cobblestones towards the edge of town. On one side of Northgate were several brick mansions, exactly alike except that a few had iron railings or enclosed recesses in front. Nora Lofts, noted author of historical fiction, wrote often of these East Anglian residences, whose large recesses were at one time used as entrances for horse and carriage. The seventeenth-century buildings have endured many years of human life with famines, drought, war and plague, and are now converted into high ceiling modern homes with lovely enclosed gardens.

Never in my wildest dreams did I think that thirty-six years later we would be having Sunday dinner at The Angel in Bury St. Edmunds with our son David, his delightful wife, Jan (a native of Clackmannanshire, Scotland), and our two beautiful red-headed grandchildren, Madeline and Callum, the latter of which was proudly boasting a broken arm. David has lost his Texas twang now that he lives in Suffolk to the east of Bury, where he is an information scientist for British Telecom, a vast telephone corporation. The Angel has survived many changes over the centuries, but from the ancient Abbey Gate, it still has a feeling of magnificence. In 1986, instead of dinner in a formal dining room, we were led down worn stone steps to what must have been the wine cellar at one time. It definitely was not a "kids eat free" fast-food place. The Angel had seemed very expensive in 1950—but thirty-six years later, it was unreal!

Rain. And more rain. The weather in East Anglia was fascinating. Within an hour, summer storms lived and died and the sun shone bright again. Tiny pubs were scattered conveniently along the roads and we stopped often for tea and pastries, or sometimes weak English ale. We continued to Stowmarket and spent the night in another rather expensive—17/16—nineteenth-century hotel. I mentioned to the clerk how picturesque the natural-colored thatched roofs were on the wattle-and-daub country homes. He told us that thatch, made from turves, straw, bracken or whatever, was getting too expensive. As it wore off, the roofs were being replaced by red tile.

Most of the cottages had an artful charm of assorted peonies, blue cornflowers and Canterbury bells. Sweet peas crawled happily over broken fences and climbing roses covered the doorways. Hedgerows were gradually replaced by walls of unmortared stones balanced by gravity and friction. Winding stone walls meandered for miles, threading into odd shaped boundaries along deeply worn country roads which at one time must have been used as packhorse trails.

I cycled happily along with the wind at my back. This was truly a no-frill farmland area with newly-plowed fields and the fresh smell of spring. The narrow back road we traveled seemed to be unsuitable for vehicles, but we plummeted right along. Innumerable wild flowers had sprung up on limestone cliffs and my bicycle was suddenly being escorted by flocks of butterflies—white and yellow—dancing overhead and all around. They flew ahead in a concerted movement, soaring up into the air or dipping between us with great swiftness. My thoughts were not on the many miles we'd traveled or how many hills we'd climbed and palaces we'd visited. I remember thinking this single experience could represent my whole life—following Hank like the sun, but every now and then, moving into my own cloud of butterflies—darting and dancing, sometimes rushing on ahead but always returning. I cycled leisurely on, oblivious of the sign: COLCHESTER, STRAIGHT AHEAD.

"Slow down. We turn here," Hank called. "We're not going to Colchester. That road would take us back toward London!"

We stopped, and with great patience, he unfolded his map and pointed to Manningtree, the village where we were to turn toward Harwich and the Channel. We would board the night ferry for the Hook of Holland.

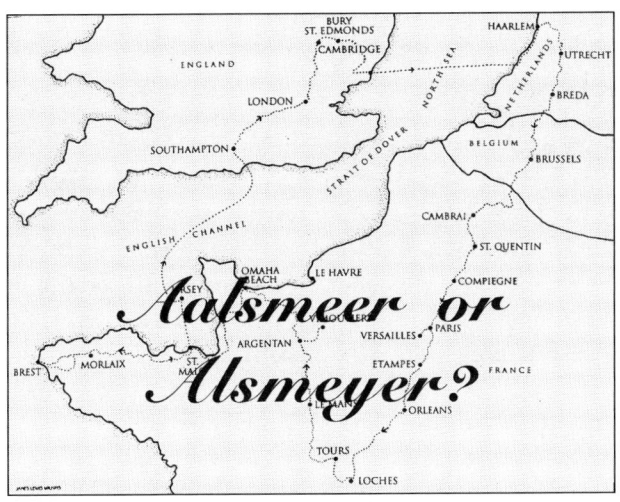

$\mathcal{I}$t was easy cycling over flat paths cut between grassy fields covered with innumerable flowers near the coastal town of Harwich. An outside display at a small greengrocer's overflowed with red strawberries, cheese, bread and apples. We bought enough to eat on the night steamer to the Hook of Holland, on the coast to the west of Rotterdam. Elderly couples, young families with anxious children, tourists, businessmen, backpackers and several cyclists were waiting patiently to be checked aboard the large ferry. After storing our bicycles deep in the hold, we settled in folding chairs for the 120-mile crossing.

Our ferry, *The Amsterdam*, was built by John Brown Ltd. of Glasgow, the builder of the *Queens*. On this June 18, the ship was on her fourth voyage across the Channel and everything glistened and smelled of newness. A strange parade of passengers marched back and forth before us. One distinguished-looking British gentleman on his way to the dining area stared at us and grumbled, "Just look at those crazy Frenchies!" And why not, I asked myself, as I took another bite from my big juicy apple; the French people often

131

thought we were English! A middle-aged woman in a fur coat sat in the recliner next to us and talked about her family's plan to rent a new 1949 Packard and travel through all of the Netherlands and several other countries in only ten days. Ten days! I didn't envy her a bit! Several students were taking advantage of the special rail rates for "Anywhere in the country, five dollars for five days." A bargain, but I still preferred cycling.

The sun rose slowly above the foggy horizon as *The Amsterdam* pulled alongside the dock. It took an hour to get our bicycles out of the hold and clear customs. Soon we were cycling north through thick fog, but we stopped for pastries and coffee when drizzle gradually turned to rain. Even at this early morning hour, workmen were sitting at tables conveniently covered with wrapping paper. During each hint of rain—and there were many—we stopped for coffee and fattening waffle-like pastries dripping with whipped cream.

Amsterdam is the legal capital of Holland, although the Dutch have trouble trying to explain to foreigners that most political action takes place in The Hague. The harbor connects with the North Sea by a broad canal, and southward across the flat land is Schiphol Airport, home of the KLM System which was slowly being rebuilt into one of Europe's most important airlines. Germans razed the airport in 1945.

The country is truly flat, with canals used for barges and ice skating, while dikes keep out the sea and windmills pump off excess water. Actually, the greatest flood in Holland since the thirteenth century was a man-made catastrophe in 1945 when German forces opened the dikes that protected Wieringermeer polder. It became a 50,000-acre lake which took the Dutch a year to pump dry. One-fifth of Holland lies below sea level and there are plans to reclaim even more land from the old Zuyder Zee. The Dutch have been reclaiming land from the sea since the Middle Ages and have become quite expert at it.

I had never seen so many windmills. Wind-driven water pumps stood out like great giants waiting for Don Quixote. Not until they were invented were the Dutch able to pump the Zee dry on any large scale. Before then, water drained from low-lying fields was bailed out with buckets and dumped on the sea side of the dike. Even though most water pumps are now powered by electricity, there are still more than 13,000 fat wooden windmills churning away slowly in the constant wind.

Hank located on his map the village of Spaarnvan only a few kilometers off the main highway between the Hook and Haarlem. His "detour" took us to a small statue of the famous little boy who stuck his finger in the hole of a dike. Everyone knows the familiar story, but the statue was new when we visited. According to the European edition of *Time*, this "Hero of Haarlem" statue had been unveiled only the previous week by Princess Margriet, who dedicated it to ". . . our youth, to honor the boy who symbolized the perpetual struggle of Holland against the water."

The sky turned dark, and curdled clouds covered a depressing sky as we cycled into Haarlem in mid-afternoon. It turned out to be one of those typically dull and sullen spring days when wind from the North Sea whips rain into the ground and empties the crowded streets. We stopped for coffee and waited, for we knew if we waited long enough, the sun would eventually shine again. It was misting along the coast when we passed through villages which at one time had been prosperous seaports, long before the Zuyder Zee became an inland lake. Snug houses were nestled closely behind the dikes and pink-faced old gentlemen in baggy trousers waved to us as they smoked their pipes along the docks.

Food was not being rationed, but a waiter told us that meat was forbidden on Tuesdays and Thursdays. He also laughed and said he thought all Americans drank only Coca-Cola. Even though our rather plain seafood dinner was not expensive, when Hank pulled out his wallet, we became quickly aware of our depressing financial status. Our account back home, I reminded him, should have increased by about $200 since our departure. We still had one War Bond, plus about $35 from the weekly newspaper features and my last paycheck, which included $45 teacher's retirement that I didn't know I was eligible for! Before we left Haarlem, I wrote a "Dear Dad" letter asking him to withdraw the money and send a check for $300 via American Express in Paris by July 1. This was a new experience for all of us. (Remember: This was before the days of plastic cards!) I cautioned Dad to include Hank's full name, as written on our passport, to sign the checks in all the necessary places and to keep a copy of the check numbers. As soon as we received the money, we would be able to make reservations for return passage in September after six weeks in Switzerland. Hank worried whether a G. I. Bill check for $300 would be enough, but I reminded him that my friend Tut who had been in Fribourg the previous summer assured us that our check from the Veterans Administration would easily cover expenses.

"He'd better be correct!" Hank said, looking through his wallet. "The newspaper reports that students rank second in 147 occupational groups among U.S. tourists to Europe this summer. Students are predicted to spend about eight percent of the total expenditures by dollar-carrying tourists. That's about $16,500,000 excluding ship passage. It also says that half of the students crossed the Atlantic on freighters, while others traveled first class on passenger steamers and a few by plane. I guess you could say we are quite typical."

The next day we cycled by cathedral-like brick churches squeezed into almost every small village. Even the countryside was sprinkled with huge ornate churches topped by tall steeples. One large tower had an elaborate belfry where chimes played every hour, causing an archangel to blow his trumpet and a knight on horseback to gallop across a window-like opening below.

Holland's tradition of religious liberty goes back to the Reformation. Calvinism took an early hold in this country and many religious refugees from England, including our Pilgrim fathers, found refuge in the Netherlands before sailing to the New World. There was still a damp bleakness in the older sanctuaries, and in some areas there were signs warning that women are still required to dress "in a way so not to be sexually appealing." Photos were not allowed in some churches because the people believe the Bible means literally what it says: "Thou shalt not make any graven images."

We paid four guilders—$1.50—for a B&B and again cycled on the right hand side of the roads, leisurely covering fifty miles or so in a single day. Hard showers and cold winds continued to break suddenly into clear blue skies and sunshine, making the weather very unpredictable. The rain left an awful stench in ditches. We became very conscious of rough cobblestone, as nuts and bolts literally flew from my bicycle. When something fell off, usually the chain unwound from the sprockets and the whole thing stopped working. I would give a distressing "HEEE-HAAAW," but by the time Hank came to help, I would have already replaced the nuts or whatever fell off. It was no easy task, fitting cogs to the sprocket every hour or so. I had thought at first it was ridiculous to carry a small packet of basic tools and an air pump, but in Holland I realized they were vital pieces of equipment.

Hank studied his maps closely, trying to decide whether to cycle to Alkmaar or Aalsmeer. There was also "Asmer," but it was to the east a considerable distance. In Alkmaar, we read, we could tour colorful markets where shining round cheese in the shape and size of overgrown oranges is carried to old weight-houses by white-clad porters in brilliant beribboned hats. Fascinating, yes, but we chose Aalsmeer because of the familiar sounding name. Aalsmeer is a busy city in the heart of the great Dutch flower growing district between Haarlem and Utrecht. Some 15,000 acres of bulbs form immense carpets of color across the flat earth. Central Aalsmeer Auction Mart, the largest flower market in the Netherlands, was actually only a small village surrounded by acres of hothouses and

Odd-shaped "barn" at Aalsmeer.

Wind-powered crane storing hay.

flowering fields laced by narrow canals. Much of the area is polder, land reclaimed by draining lakes.

We met Mr. G. A. Vos, the overseer, who took us on a tour of the gymnasium-like building. The history of the tulip's arrival in Holland is shrouded in myth and mystique, he said. As the Dutch tell their story, it was in 1593 when the Austrian ambassador to the old Ottoman Empire was so taken by a flower he saw in the sultan's court that he sent some bulbs to a Dutch botanist, who planted them in his garden in Leiden. The next year, the first tulip bloomed in Dutch soil.

The huge flower mart was divided by a canal through the center. Almost buried under loads of flowers, thirty-foot barges powered by outboard motors converged on the scene from a web of canals. Trucks and horsedrawn carts brought even more flowers.

Inside the Central Aalsmeer Auction Mart.

Auctions for over six million flower samples are held all year long with sales every day in one of the five auction rooms where flowers are brought. Bids come fast. A complicated electrical device, something like an eight-foot clock face mounted on a pinball machine, made the click of blinking lights the only sound to be heard. Buyers punched lighted buttons to make their bids and the auctioneer merely recorded the sales. Buyers pay cash; credit is not a familiar word around Aalsmeer.

Near the end of the recent war, Mr. Vos said, Aalsmeer was cut off from outside food supplies by German occupation troops, forcing many people to eat tulip bulbs to keep from starving. By the time of our visit, of course, the people had returned to raising bulbs for ornamental use and were planning a gigantic rally in a few weeks.

While having lunch in a small restaurant at the edge of Utrecht, a Dutch youth heard us talking about a huge boulder attached by a heavy chain to a nearby stone bridge. He came to our table and said with a wide grin, "I speak English, yes? You have seen our boulder chained to the bridge?" He turned to the local people at the next table. "The Devil made them do it, yes?" Townspeople leaned towards the young man, waiting to hear again the familiar tale. "Many years ago the people of Utrecht had a problem. A *big* problem." He then told us that it was not high taxes or bombs, but a problem created by the Devil himself. Centuries ago, the story goes, during one of the Devil's most playful moments, he and his friend would take a boulder from under the bridge and toss it back and forth across the canal. The Devil could handle the stone as easily as a tennis ball but his friend was less agile. Whenever he dropped the stone into the canal, there was a rumbling that shook the entire village of Utrecht. To keep it from happening again, brave villagers took heavy chains and fastened the boulder to the bridge.

"Even Satan himself cannot move it," the youth said proudly. "True? Maybe yes. Maybe no . . . ." he said with a twinkle in his blue eyes. The small audience clapped and insisted it actually happened.

Since arriving in Holland Hank noticed that his tendency to stray from the *beaten* path was matched by my taking advantage of the *eaten* path. His empty wallet proved it. (By the time we returned to Texas, I had gained 10 or 12 pounds, all muscle and pommes frites.) I ate everything I saw except the tiny eels that squirmed around one over the other at the fishmonger's shop. Their long wormlike bodies had smooth slimy skin flattening out at the tail; some were transparent and crawled around in the window containers like tiny snakes. Hank jumped off the sidewalk the first time we passed the fishmonger's window. His everlasting fear of snakes comes from boyhood memories of summers spent on his grandfather's southeast Texas rice farm, inhabited by many snakes, some venomous.

I joined a group of Dutch people waiting at a tram stop who were buying herring for a nickel at a little sidewalk stand. The vendor showed me the art of swallowing the little things. Whole. Simply pick it up by the tail, drag it through a sauce of chopped onions, then put it into your mouth. Simple, but messy. A towel was nailed to a post to wipe my fingers on. Herring is quite delicious, even though the method of eating was not too sanitary. Hank wouldn't even watch.

He would go to the next vendor and buy tiny weenies, huge pickles and tons of fried potatoes.

In Utrecht, Hank bought two more maps. His Royal Dutch Shell map was the *Wegenkaart van Nederland.* A Pneu Michelin map was for *Amsterdam, Bruxelles, Paris, Hollande-Belgique-Luxembourg-Nord de France.* We wanted to see more of Utrecht, the site of the signing of the Treaty of Utrecht in 1713, which is important to the history of Europe, as well as England and America. From here, we planned to cycle to Gorinchem, cross the Rhine and then continue south to Breda and on into Belgium. This was a big decision, prompted in part because we found the Netherlands far too expensive. I was a bit disappointed, for earlier we had hoped to visit the area where the great Impressionist painter Vincent van Gogh had lived. The woman at the Dutch Tourist Office in Paris had even told

Flat roads of the Netherlands.

us the proper way to pronounce Van Gogh's name by making a deep guttural sound like clearing your throat then spitting: Von ch-HO-o-o-k-k. Strange, but actually, it does sound quite authentic.

Holland and northern Belgium were interesting and great for cycling. Take the village of Gorinchem, for instance. It has mirrors uniquely placed above doorways of homes and small shops, allowing the person on the second floor to see who has rung the doorbell below! The countryside was filled with numerous flat-bottomed, heavy-breasted barges, drawing only a few feet of water as they nudged through narrow gateways with great confidence. Most were guided by fat-bottomed, heavy-breasted women in flying aprons and wooden shoes who hung washing on the foremast like a new signaling system. Some barges had elaborate scroll work on the hulls and intricately carved tillers. Bicycles leaned against cabin walls. Motor-driven barges crawled slowly through canals, climbing up lock by lock. A few rowboats were staked at convenient spots in front of businesses that opened directly onto the canals. Horses walked along worn paths pulling smaller barges, and almost everyone waved to us as we cycled by. We noticed that Dutch bicycles were built with handlebars raised high, allowing riders to sit erect.

Going south from Utrecht, Hank recorded in his journal that fittingly enough, on June 21, the longest day of the year, we made what was likely our longest distance cycled in a single day. Unfortunately, and uncharacteristically, he failed to note just how many kilometers it was! The flat country had convenient four-lane bicycle paths bordering the highways.

Only once did we have difficulty with both language and money. It was at a small pastry shop when Hank gave the young waitress a small silver guilder.

"No! No!" she said, pushing it back towards him.

"Not enough?" Hank asked, handing her more coins. "No! No! Too precious!" she said again. She held the coin so Hank could read the date on it—1892—and see a picture of a very young girl with long hair.

"No. No. No. Queen Wilhelmina. Young girl. Long hair! Guilder very very old. You must keep for yourself. Take to America," she insisted. Later, I read that the coin was historically important because Wilhelmina became queen of The Netherlands in 1890 when her father William III died. When Germans invaded her country in 1940, they failed to capture her before she escaped to London. From there, she directed the war until her people could welcome her home again. The coin has become even more valuable since she died in 1949.

Hank tried to get her to take it anyway, but she refused. He reluctantly pulled another coin from his pocket and gave it to her.

The quarter-size guilder, dated 1892, with the picture of Holland's young long-haired princess on it, is now over a hundred years old. It is still in my box of treasures.

Bridges over canals in Utrecht.

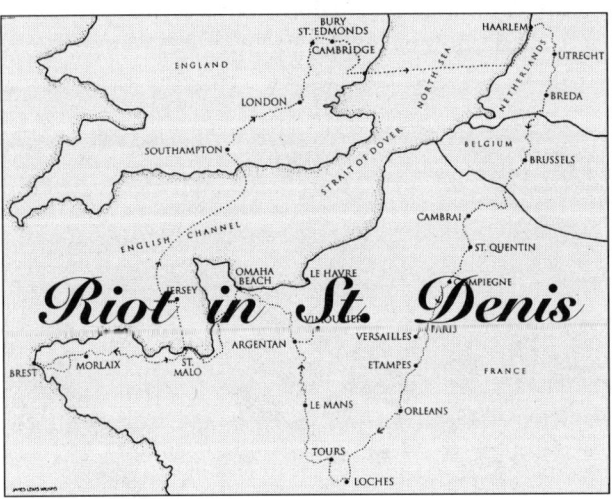

Riot in St. Denis

$\mathcal{H}$ank carefully studied his maps of The Netherlands and prepared his next "Seeing Europe" article. I looked over his shoulder a few minutes, knowing my letters to mother usually related to other things than did his carefully prepared features. But she didn't mind. I continued to send her neat handwritten feature stories Hank wrote, she would transcribe them on her little portable typewriter and put the copy in the mail to area newspapers. By this time in our journey, it was almost unbelievable how quickly the time had passed. It seemed only yesterday that we left Paris and began cycling—seemingly always uphill—through Normandy and Brittany. Ordinary irritations that go with routines of home—paying bills, laundry, dishes and dusting—were long forgotten as I laid back and thought of the people we'd met and the places we'd been.

A heavy gate and a wire fence were the only things we found dividing Belgium from the Netherlands. A customs agent stood nearby, smoking a cigarette. "America?" he asked in a bored voice.

"Yes. From Texas," Hank answered as I dug through my purse for our green passport and other identification. Fortunately, the

At the Belgian border.

sticky international red tape that usually takes an hour or more to complete did not unravel here. After a quick glance at my little wicker basket and Hank's blue camera box and saddlebags, he returned our passport with a simple rubber stamp imprint. There was no complicated currency form to fill in, nor did the customs agents peer into Hank's wallet, as they had in Southampton.

Belgium's geographical position has for a thousand years made the country a battleground of western Europe as well as a trading post for all the world. English woolen goods, Oriental fabrics, Russian furs and Flemish wines pass through Belgian ports. American-made automobiles roar along century-old streets passing an amazing array of shops selling antique housewares alongside the latest American-made products. Coffee was sometimes as much as fifteen cents a cup and other food was priced accordingly; American magazines sold for double the marked price. Everyone seemed well dressed. Small whitewashed houses with uneven green slate roofs were grouped around neat town squares. Green lawns covered with yellow daffodils and flowering trees looked as if they had been patted into place hundreds of years ago and never disturbed.

The countryside looked more like the rolling hills near Paris than the polders of Holland, and the people had darker hair instead of the harsh blondness of the Dutch. Belgians in the north speak Flemish and in the south, French and Walloon, an old French dialect. We had little trouble with our "Americanese."

Belgium must have been heavily damaged during World War II but we did not cycle through those areas. It is said that nearly every great European power has at one time or another occupied Belgium and tried to "discipline" it, usually without success. That was especially true when Germany attacked the country without warning in 1940. Within two weeks, King Leopold III surrendered and was taken prisoner. The Belgium Cabinet refused to give up, however, and like Queen Wilhemina, fled to London and became the Belgium government-in-exile. Only historians will be able to record the disasters they endured, especially during the final Battle of the Bulge. As we cycled along, it was unbelievably quiet, but even so, the smallest villages were working to rebuild crumbling buildings.

We breezed around the edge of Antwerp and spent the night in Malines, an ancient city famous for ornate lace and furniture-making. It also had tough police control. Crossing the border had been simple enough, but it was not so easy in Malines. In a dimly lit hotel lobby, we had to fill in two long forms, in duplicate, listing everything from birth dates to why and where we were traveling and how much cash we had.

"You must leave your passport at the desk," the clerk said in stilted English.

"Why?" Hank asked, as he handed it back to me. "It is required by law. A police officer must check it on his evening inspection," the clerk replied. Hank refused.

"I am only trying to save you the inconvenience of being wakened near midnight," the clerk insisted. "I assure you, the police *will* check the register here and he *will* knock on your door before the night is over."

"I'll keep it anyway," Hank repeated. We stored our bicycles and climbed very narrow stairs to an attic room overlooking the town square. As expected, about midnight we heard the sound of heavy boots followed by a knock on the door.

"Police!" came a loud voice from the hallway. I slid farther beneath the soft down comforter while Hank opened the door a crack.

"Yes?" Hank asked sleepily.

"Your passport, please," the uniformed policeman demanded harshly, pushing the door open with his heavy boot. Hank handed it to him. He studied it closely, then whispered something to a man in plain clothes waiting in the hallway.

"He wants to know your wife's maiden name," the second man explained.

"Maiden name? Why?" I asked, poking my head from the covers. "It's the law," the man replied firmly.

"Bennett. Marie Bennett," Hank said. The man wrote it on a slip of paper and handed it to the officer. They both bowed and thanked us profusely before hurrying down the hallway to knock on another door. So ended our first night in Belgium.

Construction on the town hall in Malines was begun long ago, but only during the occupation of the First World War did the Belgians finish it, mostly to keep everyone busy and avoid deportation. Compared with the heavy thick Dutch churches, the massive St. Mombaud Cathedral is quite beautiful. They claim it has the most famous carillons in all of Europe, said to weigh nine tons. Religious symbols seem to be nationally recognized. If a lamp is placed upside down, it means a foolish virgin; an ordinary lamp, Jesus Christ; a sword, martyrdom; and a pelican tearing its breast, the symbol of redemption. Many other medieval observances are still actively attended.

The small palace built by Mary of Austria was being used as a Palace of Justice. A guide took us through a narrow doorway and down a short flight of stairs. "This area was originally built to dispose of people of whom the queen disapproved," he said. "It was once deadly to be sent here. However, judges now make better use of it." With great flourish, he opened a heavy vault-like door to expose a neat row of hats and heavy coats hanging from the wall.

The sun came out as we left so we joined a group of children and parents in the park. They had gathered to see a puppet show, a delightful combination of Caesar, Charlemagne, and Napoleon, all participating at once.

The next morning we continued towards Brussels, a beautiful city that lies almost in the center of Belgium. It is divided into Upper Town and Lower Town, and there is a definite difference in their way of life. Lower town was noisier, stores were smaller and they were less expensive. There were fewer neon lights and automobiles. As we arrived lightning danced between dark storm clouds, followed by rumbles of thunder before it began to rain. A few laborers at a lumberyard motioned us inside their shelter until the storm blew over. We didn't stay long because Hank was anxious to locate a small hotel along Gare du Nord where he and friends had stayed in 1946. The only other thing he could remember about the city is that one museum had several paintings by Van Dyck and Reubens and a small replica of New York City's Times Square. Unfortunately, the museum was closed on that Friday afternoon. The day wasn't wasted, for we cycled the narrow crooked streets lined with medieval houses in the rain. We saw, in various stages of repair, a large number of government buildings that had been severely damaged during the war. Canals flowed quietly below old aristocratic buildings and markets seemed to be plentiful in a still-hungry Europe. Constant drizzle kept me from getting a picture of the 300-year-old uninhibited statue of a small boy relieving himself in the most convenient way.

We ate waterzooi de poulet—rice soup with chicken and potatoes—at an inexpensive family-style restaurant. Not bad. The son waited on the tables, the father took the money and the daughter worked in the kitchen with her mother. Cycling through Brussels during morning rush was no easy task, and even Hank had to admit we were lost several times. It took us almost an hour to reach the southernmost edge of the city. On one street, very narrow and winding, we slowly pushed our loaded bicycles uphill over rough bricks. Horns honked. Bells rang. Cars crept by slowly in the opposite direction. Drivers yelled angrily and pointed to a street sign: a big white circle with a red border and a red slash through it. A policeman hurriedly shoved us out of the way of a reckless driver, yelling that we were "Dumb Danes" and several unquotable names. One-way? Oh? Ooooooh.

We were glad to reach the Flemish countryside. Only hard work has kept the land from returning to rivers and marshes; the countryside seems to sleep in its own amazing beauty. A few kilometers to the east across dull green and brown fields is the site of the Battle of Waterloo. We cycled seventy kilometers to Mons near the French border and visited the scene of the British Expeditionary Force's first mounted charge against the Germans in World

Marie Bennett Alsmeyer in front of monument to British Expeditionary Force's first mounted charge against the Germans during WWI.

War I. A granite monument with a plaque marked the site of the first casualty.

Crossing the border into France somehow made me feel as if we were going home. We stopped at a tiny restaurant along the border. The waitress, a heavyset woman in a white apron, insisted on telling us her most exciting World War II experience. We expected to hear tales of being caught in the midst of battle, surrounded by army tanks and gunfire at close range. Or maybe she had worked with the French Underground. No, she said, her most memorable event was when American army troops marched down the street and she shook hands with a famous Hollywood movie star, a handsome lieutenant from America named "Robert" somebody.

War damages again became quite evident as we cycled into Mauberge for the night. Suffering was obviously nothing new, as fortifications had first been built there hundreds of years ago. Because of the terrible cobblestone streets, my bicycle chain kept slipping off, until finally, it could take no more torment and fell to the ground in two pieces. I was left pedaling fast but going no place. This must not have been unusual in this area, however, for we had no trouble finding a man at a repair shop to replace it.

Our hotel was a postwar temporary wooden structure. Both of us were quite shaken from the rough cobbles. I went to bed with a dull headache, the kind that makes your head explode when you cough. Just as suddenly as the sun came up the next morning, the rain stopped and my headache faded away as if by magic.

We cycled towards Cambrai that morning and stopped for a moment at a monument that was no larger than a small tombstone. We were fortunate to see it, for it was almost hidden beneath a pile of rubbish and a few rusty barrels and crates. The carving read: STOP. THINK AND CONSIDER THE FATE OF THOSE WHO WERE BRUTALLY SHOT HERE BY THE NAZI APRIL 8, 1944. A very sad story must lie hidden behind that almost forgotten tiny monument. We continued south and had lunch beside a large simple American Battle Memorial atop an artificial hill covering St. Quentin canal which was built during the Napoleonic years. Almost at the west base of the tunnel overhead was a part of the famed World War I Hindenburg Line. To the east, there had been intensive fighting by American troops. A short distance away, an American cemetery with more than 1,800 graves remained.

It is hard to visualize fighting in this gentle rolling countryside. Hank took a special interest in the monument commemorating units that included his father's 80th "Blue Ridge Division." They served with the British as part of the Somme offensive in August, 1918. The division was in both the Meuse-Argonne and St. Mihiel campaigns to the east in the months before Armistice Day. The St. Mihiel battle was the first distinctly American offensive of the war. Hank's father was first sergeant in a high tech army unit that drove primitive motor trucks convoying troops and transporting war materials. He was probably the only Texan in a division composed of mostly men from Virginia and Pennsylvania. The 80th was one of two American divisions that broke through the Hindenburg Line. Hank spent several minutes silently studying the large scale map inscribed into the back of the granite monument, for his father had spoken rarely of his experiences. He had no use for war.

Hank wrote in his journal that it was fifty-nine kilometers through the Oise Valley from Noyon to Compiegne. Exactly fifty-nine? I asked. Of course! We continued through the beautiful forest

Hank Alsmeyer studying the monument (near Bellicourt, France) dedicated to his father's WWI "Blue Ridge Division."

where centuries ago kings and noblemen hunted. To the east is Soissons, a name which evokes many horror stories of trench fighting during World War I. We cycled farther south towards Compiègne where in 1918 on the eleventh hour of the eleventh day of the eleventh month, documents to end World War I were signed. Frenchmen were working on a bronze monument to replace the railroad car in which the signing had taken place. In 1940, Germans moved the wooden car to Berlin where it was eventually destroyed in an allied air raid. All that is left of this historic place is a short straight road to a narrow landscaped area that slices through a deep forest. The only other visitor was a civilian who insisted he had been an army master sergeant during World War II. He grumbled because the boxcar was no longer there.

The Oise Valley from Noyon to Compiègne had surprisingly high bluffs with sharp cliffs rising up two hundred feet or more. We stopped for the night in Verberie, and the next day began climbing the steep hills of France again. We soon came to a small cemetery with about 500 old crosses from World War I and a few freshly painted wooden crosses placed there in 1940 after the Germans rushed through that area. A few English soldiers of World War I were also buried there. Their graves, marked with weatherworn gray tombstones bearing regimental symbols of the soldier, all looked too small. Stones for French North Africans had scripts in Arabic. A few of the World War II grave markers had pictures of the deceased; typical young soldiers—handsome, smiling, and much too young to die. The grass was spongy between the rows of crosses but at least one person had been concerned enough to place artificial flowers, now limp and faded, on the graves marked simply "inconnu." Unknown.

In a neat wooded area alongside the highway was a large monument dedicated to Marshal Ferdinand Foch. His military strategy became famous during the first war for he had made a great impression on the Allied forces for his strong will and optimism. In 1918, he was placed in supreme command of all British, French, Italian, Portuguese, and American forces in France.

Before Hank could take my picture near the stone structure, I had to turn my worn brown skirt around, back to front. Why? he asked. Because the seat of my bicycle had worn a substantial hole in it. That's why!

Our last stop before arriving in Draveil was in St. Denis, a working class suburb on the northern outskirts of Paris where some of the buildings predate Notre Dame Cathedral. Visiting St. Denis proved to be among the more memorable events of the trip. The floor of the front entrance of the small hotel was covered with a worn carpet made of surplus war material showing faded collar insignias from a supply training outfit. Our room on the second floor overlooked the noisy people on the streets. Unlike most places we had been, the people here were poorly dressed and seemed quite angry at the world.

Before dinner, we visited the lovely cathedral famous for its spidery framework of stone and beautiful thick glass windows in deep reds, blues and greens. A few pieces of eleventh-century glass remained in one of the crypts. The medieval tombs are unique, with

Heading "home" to Paris.

their carved animals; a lion represents strength and a dog means fidelity. In the Renaissance era the crypts had sculptured figures of the deceased kings which well represented the cadaver. The remains of Louis XVI and his Marie and others who came along after the French Revolution are still in caskets in a fairly large crypt.

It was late when we hurried back to the hotel. Suddenly we found ourselves surrounded by an angry crowd of French Communists carrying "Ban the Bomb" signs and posters along with an abundance of Picasso's rather strange dove artwork that later became the symbol for peace. It seemed at that moment we had been out of touch with the world too long. As the month of June was ending, the world news had turned frightening. There was talk that developments in Korea might lead to another war. Pushing our way through the crowd, we went quickly to our room, from which we watched a thousand or more people milling about on the sidewalks below. A stringent voice over loud speakers called Americans "racist warmongers." About three squads of riot police arrived to bolster police forces. They made their way through the streets to keep the rioters from jamming the area. What a helpless feeling it was to hear the crowd's frantic screams and not be able to read the words in the big black headlines in the French newspapers.

Early the next morning, Hank hurried to buy a newspaper. Even though President Truman had announced that the world was closer to peace than it had been in five years, a survey by the Gallup Poll showed that most Americans expected war.

Forty-two years later, on June 4, 1992, this headline appeared in the Dallas Morning News: *"Saint-Denis: Many fear the city could be hit by violence this summer." And so it goes . . . .*

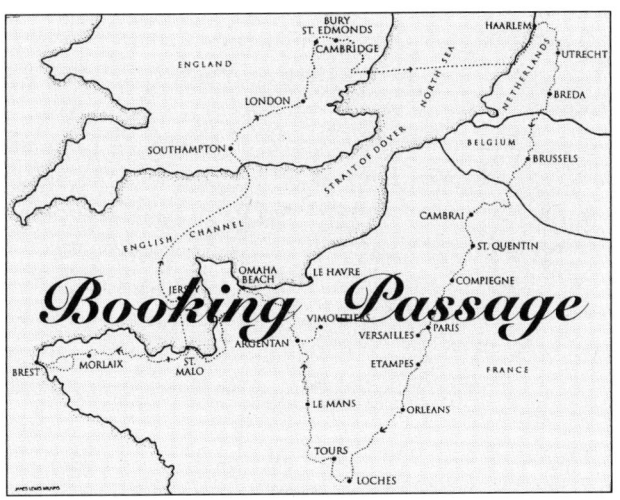

Booking Passage

        It was typical July weather, a real scorcher as we call it in Texas, but surprisingly easy cycling around the outskirts of Paris from St. Denis to Draveil on the east. We arrived about noon and while Mary was preparing lunch, Mme. Bruneteau burst in, insisting we stay in "our" flat until we could leave for Switzerland. Hank hated telling them that because of the Korean situation, we planned to book passage for New Orleans instead. The two women were well aware of the unrest throughout Korea and the world, and though disappointed, they agreed it was wise to get home before everything fell apart again.

        "I do hate to see you leave," Mme. Bruneteau said.

        "This means you will not be able to attend the University of Fribourg!" Mary said with tears in her eyes. "Hasn't your government already paid your fees?"

        "No," Hank answered. "They only issued us cards which we would have exchanged for official enrollment. I think it was about $20 for the registration and $80 tuition."

"Well, that's a large amount of money! You will just have to come back again!" Mme. Bruneteau said. "Remember, your room will be waiting for you!"

Early the next morning, we walked to Juvisy across the Seine to board the fast train to Paris. Although most Parisians seemed more concerned about the extremely hot weather than they were about world affairs, they still crowded near newsstand bulletin boards, reading the latest headlines.

First, we went to the main office of American Express to pick up our mail from home. They also had passenger information for several shipping lines, but as expected there were no openings. We joined a group of raunchy students—English, Scandinavian, Spanish and of course, American. The lobby was filled with scuffed leather luggage, bicycles, canvas backpacks and bedrolls. American Express personnel, like doting parents, comforted those who were homesick or had lost their passports, meanwhile arranging tours, train tickets, and hotel reservations for the noisy group. They handled lost-and-found items, cashed checks and distributed mail. They could handle everything, it seemed, except two tickets to board a freighter to New Orleans.

Clerks at the Lykes Lines were also discouraging, but offered to contact their Rotterdam office. Nothing. Finally we walked a few blocks farther to Waterman Lines. No openings, the clerk said politely, but asked us to wait until he contacted their London office by teletype. Sorry, he said, their two vacancies were filled this morning.

There were several other choices. We could sail to New York instead of New Orleans and save $40, but the train fare to Texas would be much more costly. Or we could go back to our original plans and attend the University of Fribourg for six weeks and hope that the international affairs would calm down. Too many decisions! It was hot and sultry, but as street lights flicked on, the city suddenly changed to its typical bustling night life. Young boys waved the disturbing headlines as they hawked their newspapers on the sidewalks.

"What should we do?" I mumbled, thinking about our finances.

"Simple," Hank replied. "We'll just buy today's *Herald Tribune*, go to a sidewalk cafe and have a glass of wine."

He read the heavy black headlines while I worried about Hank's billfold that would be virtually empty after we purchased our return passage. He carefully folded the paper when we left so he could share it with a friend of Mary's. Because of the exorbitant price, only a single copy of the American newspaper was delivered to the newsstand in Draveil each day. Hank shared his one indulgence with Mme. Bessieres, an American woman who has lived in Draveil with her French husband for a number of years. The Bessieres had invited him to dinner several times while at Orly Field.

Another day. Another 300 francs for two train tickets from Juvisy, this time to the Cosmopolitan Line office, an agent of the Consortium Maritime Franco-American Company at 1 Bis Cite Paradis. By July 6, our luck had finally changed. The clerk said he had a cancellation on a sleek new Norwegian motor ship, the *Lista*. Fare would be $200 each, plus a five dollar French embarkation tax. Would we take it? Of course! We were now scheduled to sail from Le Havre on July 12, arriving in New York City in only nine days. Our cabin would have a private bath, something I looked forward to with great anticipation! We again waited in line at American Express, this time to purchase train tickets from New York to Dallas, saving fifteen percent U.S. federal transportation tax. Every nickel counted now.

I then had to convince Hank that he desperately needed a haircut. While I wandered through book stalls along the river, he found a small barbershop on a side street. When the pudgy little barber learned Hank had been in Paris soon after the war, he began telling his own experiences as a German Prisoner of War. The more excited he got, the more red hair he cut. After an hour, Hank came out looking very very GI.

The weather turned cool and wet during our last few days in Draveil. I enjoyed the sound of the skittish pats of rain as it fell gently from the slate roof to the cobbles below.

Sounds, more than anything, have continued a thread from memory to memory, sewing patchwork scenes into the overwhelming presence of Paris in the springtime, sad remnants of wartorn beaches, London through the laughing eyes of Mrs. Philips, windmills and tulips, and especially our friends, the Grillets.

Hank brought out his journals to show Mary that the only time we were correctly identified as Americans was when we crossed the border to Belgium. In Paris and Morlaix, we were thought to be English, until someone noticed we did not use cream in our tea. Others said we looked like Canadians even though we have a German name, and in Brussels, a policeman called us "Dumb Danes." French railway stickers on our "foreign" bicycles convinced some that we were from France. Only when we spoke were they convinced we couldn't be anything but Texans.

I had only a few things to show Mary: a pair of dainty, hand-crocheted gloves to remind me of St. Lo in Normandy, a small picture of Dutch windmills from Utrecht, and a doll for my niece. Mme. Bruneteau's friend Ramona was most interested in my English version of *Tante Marie's French Cook Book* that we bought in London, and she marked several of her favorite recipes. M. Missoux at the bicycle shop offered to buy our bicycles back, but instead, we gave them to Mme. Bruneteau and her daughter because she refused to let us pay for the flat.

Paris phones are sometimes exasperating, but after several attempts, I contacted a friend of mother's who had arrived earlier from Corpus Christi. Miss Sarah Caldwell was visiting her aunt on the Ile de Saint Louis, a small suburban island north of Notre Dame Cathedral. It is covered with narrow streets and lies in the center of the oldest part of Paris, not far from the tiny hotel where we first stayed. Through the years, it has been the home of great poets, authors and relatives of kings. Miss Caldwell took us to a delightful little restaurant that catered to the "typical American tourist." She planned to return to Corpus Christi in September after traveling through Switzerland, Belgium, Holland and Scotland. Oh to be young again, she sighed when we told her about the mysterious back roads and picturesque tiny villages we discovered.

A few days later, we were invited to a Fourth of July celebration at the American Embassy. I have no idea how or why we received the engraved invitation from Ambassador and Mrs. Bruce requesting "the pleasure of your company" from 11 A.M. to 1 P.M. at 16 Avenue Gabriel. I was quite excited. France celebrates Bastille Day on July 14—a much noisier and more elaborate affair when bands play "La Marseillaise" and everyone carries tricolored flags. But this day—the fourth day of July—belongs to all Americans in Paris. Unfortunately, we missed the train and arrived after the gates were closed, so we did not attend the celebration. No Marine guards to salute us, no firecrackers, no brass bands. No delicious American hot dogs with lots of mustard!

A week later, I packed our things very slowly for I was not anxious to say goodbye. The time had come, however, and we boarded the clumsy bus in front of Mary's home and crossed the Seine one last time. Paris's streets were bustling, for it was High Season and thousands of tourists crowded every restaurant and hotel. We left our things with the little deaf lady at the Hotel du Palais and went to the restaurant next door. A familiar waitress took us to our table by the window, then hurried to tell the owner that we were back. It seemed as if we had never left.

Early on the morning of July 11, we boarded the fast train at Gare St. Lazare for Le Havre, where the *Lista* would be waiting. The Eiffel Tower faded away in the distance, and I realized how Hank must have felt when he left Orly, for I didn't want to leave either.

"Here it is—all in a nutshell!" Hank said as he settled back in the crowded compartment and pointed to the editorial page of the paper. A small boxed-in feature succinctly described the frightening headlines.

All about us prophets are busy, reporting that 3 out of 5 experts believe that there will be no total war. Or vice versa. That nobody is in a position to make any solid predictions about what Russia will, or will not, do next. Mr. Gromyko has truculently laid an utterly false foundation for any new act of aggression that his country may decide to make. The next blow may come in Germany, or in Yugoslavia— or in Persia. Or it may come in a completely unexpected quarter. . . . Or it may not come at all.

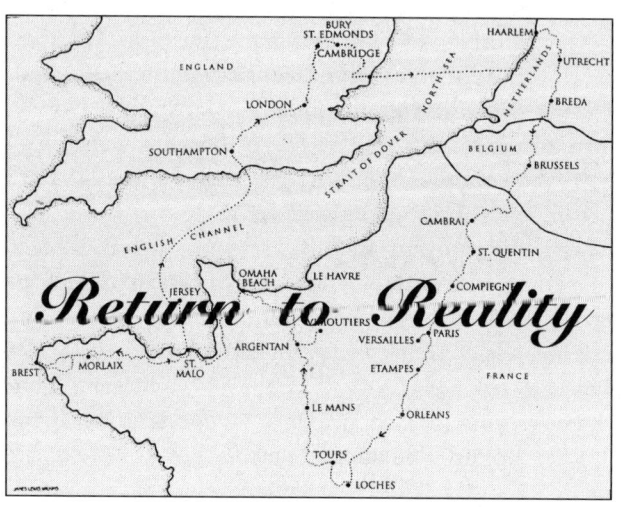

$\mathcal{C}$rossing the Atlantic on the *Pont L'Evêque* had been an experience, but returning on the *Lista* was pure luxury. The sleek white Norwegian ship was listed as a small freighter, but its passenger accommodations were excellent and obviously postwar. She was grand and dignified, even though she carried only five passengers. Captain Hagen welcomed us aboard as if we were royalty. Custom Officials went about their task of inspecting my little wicker basket, the blue metal box of camera equipment, portable typewriter, one rawhide suitcase and a couple of cardboard boxes. He asked to see our boarding pass and passport and then we signed several official papers. A boy took our boxes to the cabin and a representative of the steamship company appeared.

"You are fortunate," he said. "The *Lista* has not had to change her sailing date because of foul weather, as sometimes happens without notice this time of the year. You may consider yourselves 'fair weather sailors.'"

We remained on deck, basking in the hazy sun as it played games off a barely rippling sea. Suddenly, stray wisps of cottony clouds pushed along by the ocean breeze turned the sky dark and wicked. It began to rain and we went below. Our cabin was even nicer than expected: single beds, lots of storage, an open porthole and best of all, a private bath with shower. In the smoking lounge, we met the three other passengers: a wealthy French pianist who commuted regularly between Paris and New York; Ms. Love, a middle-aged woman wearing many diamonds and pearls but no wedding ring; and a teenage boy on his way to visit his American mother in Pennsylvania.

The Channel was a bit restless the first night. I laid in the bed listening to the wails and groans of the ship, reminding myself that the sea is not to be trifled with. What a wonderful feeling. Going home! Our ancestors crossed this same ocean two hundred or so years ago, and we accept without question their desire to seek freedom of religion, politics and economics in the "Promised Land." Often, we don't appreciate their efforts to the fullest.

During the day, I was reduced to idleness by ocean swells topped with scallops of foam, poetically called "white horses." Though the pace of the ship was sedate, I was never bored. I read a lot and enjoyed tea and scones during the afternoons. I was struck by the image of how tiny the *Lista* was compared to other liners as we got out of radio range and faced the vastness of the ocean. In the evening, light from the portholes pinpricked the darkness, and soft "Big Band" music was swept away by the soft breeze. The pianist and Ms. Love talked quietly in the corner while the teenager studied a huge wall map of the Atlantic that covered one wall. Hank traced the *Lista's* route for him.

"Actually," he told the boy, "sailing to New York from Le Havre is quite easy. See? We are now approximately forty-nine degrees latitude north, a half-degree longitude west. New York, according to this map, is forty degrees latitude north and seventy-four degrees longitude west. With the help of a compass, the captain simply marks the spot and guides the ship in that direction. Of course, there might be some changes due to foul weather. You should ask Captain Hagen to show you his equipment up on the bridge." The boy was delighted.

A couple of days passed. The sun faded away and the horizon never again pierced the soft thick fog that quickly blended into a mucky spray. Several fogbows formed nebulous arcs of white and yellow lights that faded gradually into a dull olive gauze of darkness.

Every two minutes, the ship's foghorn gave four-second BEEEee-OOooing blasts. We churned through deep fog, skirting weather troughs and frequent squalls while the ocean played mean tricks on my stomach. Soon after leaving the English Channel, I became nauseated, not by raging storms but by continuous gentle hypnotic rolls. I laid on the bed, my face to the wall. Never again would I tease Hank about his "mal de mer." He threatened to make me eat my words—if I could hold them down! I didn't even complain when he put on his field jacket and stood in a sheltered area on the deck smoking his pipe. When he came back in—with ruddy cheeks and broad smile—he told me about visiting with some of the crew. I could have cared less.

The next day I was finally able to eat something more than crackers so I went on deck to find a canvas chair in a sunny spot out of the wind. Two young stewardesses were also enjoying a bit of hazy sun nearby. They seemed to be speaking Nynorsk, a dialect spoken in the farm areas of Norway, or perhaps Riksmaal from the east, and they had a quaint accent when they spoke English. I asked if they were the "crew" Hank had been telling me about. They giggled, cutting their bright blue eyes at each other. One young lady had just washed her hair and it flew in the wind. The other wore hers plaited into a thick braid that wrapped around her head. They giggled again when I said I envied their being on this beautiful little Norwegian ship.

"You envy *us*? Aboard *this* ship, madam?"

"Indeed I do! Several years ago at the university, my roommate, Peggy, and I had visions of sailing on just such a freighter. However, American cargo vessels do not allow women to be part of the crew—not even Peggy, who is a registered nurse or me, a hospital corpsman in the Navy!"

"OOOooo, madam! That would never happen in Norway. We come from poor families and go to school in small settlements along the coast. The sea is our highway and main source of income. We must all work. In America, everyone has an education."

"Not everyone. I grew up on the Gulf Coast of Texas, and life is not always easy there, either. I often wonder what it would be like to travel around the world like you do. But Peg soon married Bert and I married Hank, the tall fellow with red hair. Have you met him yet?"

"AAHHHhhh. Yes. He talks funny and wears such big shoes," one said cutting her eyes and giggling again. "You not only have a university degree, madam, but also a tall handsome husband," the other added quickly.

"I'll have to tell him that," I said, laughing. "My friend's brother Tut spent the summer in Norway and Switzerland and told us how beautiful your country is." They chatted between themselves then began telling me about the Land of the Midnight Sun, and the fjords along the jagged coasts that sometimes reach far inland between steep cliffs. A bell rang and they quickly bowed and hurried inside to prepare the tables for dinner, giggling all the way.

COSMOPOLITAN LINE
Lista
19/7.50.
MENU

Bulliong.

Cod fillet.Hollandece.

Pork shops.Cauliflovers,French potatoes
Salad.

Pannekaker.Suzette.
Crèpes Suzette

Coffee.

At 1830:Meatkakes.Green peas steew

A menu from the Lista.

The lounge also served as the dining room. All five passengers as well as the chief engineer and first mate sat at the Captain's table. My appetite returned, but I never got accustomed to the buffet style breakfast with all sorts of cheeses and little fish. Mostly raw. I drank black coffee. Most meals were quite good, but a bit different. Menus were printed with unique Scandinavian spelling:

Cod fillet. Bulliong. Hollandece. Park shops.
Metkakes. Green peas steem Caluliflovers.
French potatoes. Pannekaker.
Crepes Suzette and coffee

As we neared the harbor in New York, thick fog lifted and the ocean was again a deep calm blue. The horizon made a perfect circle around us and the sun appeared through blustering clouds for several hours at a time. A farewell party was planned for the last evening. We met in the lounge where fancy cheeses and sparkling white champagne were served, followed by a very elaborate dinner. Each place on the white linen tablecloth was lined with crystal glasses in rows like sparkling soldiers. Sherry was served with the soup, and fish and shrimp cooked in white wine, asparagus and peas all on one huge platter and fresh-baked bread and real butter. Red wine was served with roast beef, and the salad had bits of baked chicken in it. We drank sherry again with caramel pudding, and had a choice of Cointreau, Cognac, or Benedictine with our coffee.

"A pilot boat will arrive during the night and customs officers will board at daybreak," Captain Hagen said as we stood on deck. "That is Nantucket Island in the distance. We are scheduled to dock at 9 A.M."

Early the next morning I went out on the deck. A balmy breeze messed up my hair but I didn't mind. I got a glimpse of the stately copper Statute of Liberty, a gift to the United States from France in 1884 that is exactly like the small replica we saw near a bridge in Paris. Her crown was filled with long brilliant sunrays and her arm was raised high into the sky, a symbol of true friendship. Hank and I held hands. The other passengers stood beside us—the pianist, the diamond-studded woman, and the teenaged boy. I was sorry our voyage had come to an end on this July 22, 1950, then I realized that *returning* is not the point. The point is the *crossing*. We would soon be back to basics and face reality with only two one-way train tickets to Texas and a bit of luggage. Nothing more. No money in the bank, no income, no prospects of a job. But I decided not to worry about that. As Scarlett O'Hara said, "After all, tomorrow is another day!"

It is just as well we decided to return to Texas when we did. Our son David arrived at 2:34 A.M., June 30, 1951.

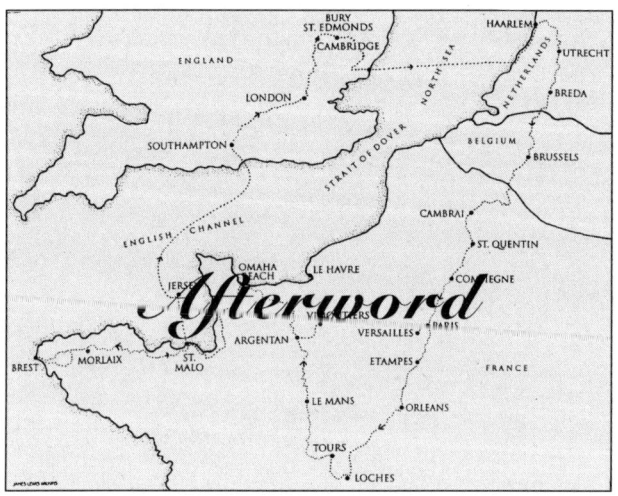

*J*ust how should a woman my age act? When my children make disparaging remarks about what I should and shouldn't do at my age, I just smile knowingly and tell them they had better use digestible words because one day they might have to eat them.

Having the desire to write the first draft of this manuscript was quite exciting and compelling, but then came the part where I had to fix it. As I sifted through papers on my desk, I often found myself remembering that unique summer. The little wicker basket is still used for family picnics, but Hank's GI field jacket is long gone. Never again will it reek of sharp Camembert cheese and french bread. Slowing the clock is a matter of rewinding the past. My letters and Hank's journals help me sort out the blur of years past, forming from the jumble a pattern of events. It was fun to compare my letters with Hank's journals, sort of like comparing my *Joy of Cooking* with his Michelin maps. Without question, Hank insists good large-scale maps have repaid their cost a thousand times over. He immerses himself in them, pores over them and insists it is time well spent. My thoughts remain in clouds of butterflies and the aroma of fresh baked bread. These differences make for a good marriage.

With the coming of the twenty-first century, I feel it is time to relive these events from my past. I can edit, embroider and punch up the experiences of forty-four years ago even though I have trouble remembering what happened to me yesterday. I can out-memory our children, for I've acquired a considerable amount of calendar! Age has given me another advantage: I find what would have been an irritating distraction at thirty has become an enjoyable detour at seventy. By now, I know where the main road ends and I'm in no particular hurry to get there. Maybe Hank is right: those roads less traveled have changed my life, and I revel in it.

I wrote this book a little at a time, putting different events into some order that link me to a completely different period in my life. I looked forward to writing time as the best part of the day. Hours or minutes—who cares?—lapse without reason. When I had done as much as I could, I would stop for a cup of coffee, run errands, or as a last resort, clean the bathroom. As I wrote it occurred to me that writing is like making sourdough bread, where you mix flour, water, sourdough starter—maybe a little salt—and you have the staff of life. The ingredients for writing are simple: a ream of paper and a floppy disk. I began recording my letters and journals on a computer that was very slow and "user friendly" only because I pampered it. My box of memories has been "leavening" for decades, my sourdough bread starter takes only a few weeks. I gather those memories—or "starter"—and lay all the ingredients before me. Dough is mixed, shaped and punched down, and I do the same with writing. Sourdough starter sometimes separates, leaving a thick glob of paste at the bottom of the container. After a bit of stirring, it becomes thick and smooth again. Rewriting is just as easy when I rethread words into smoother, more elastic sentences.

A few commas and semicolons add spice, and texture sweetens road signs or Hank's map showing inclines of $<< 12\% >>$. Dough must be punched down just as every sentence must be edited. Divide dough into loaves, sentences into paragraphs. Waiting for the results is the most difficult part, whether from the oven or the publisher.

My fingers move lightly over the keys. Out my window, a hummingbird drinks nectar, and I find myself again in East Anglia on my little blue bicycle. The aroma of warm sourdough bread comes from the kitchen. "Are you sure cycling again at seventy doesn't make sense?" I ask. "Let's try!"

Smoke from his pipe slowly curls towards the ceiling and he reaches for his box of worn Michelin maps and smiles. "Why not?" he says.

What a beautifully crazy senseless thing to do!

Yes, why not!

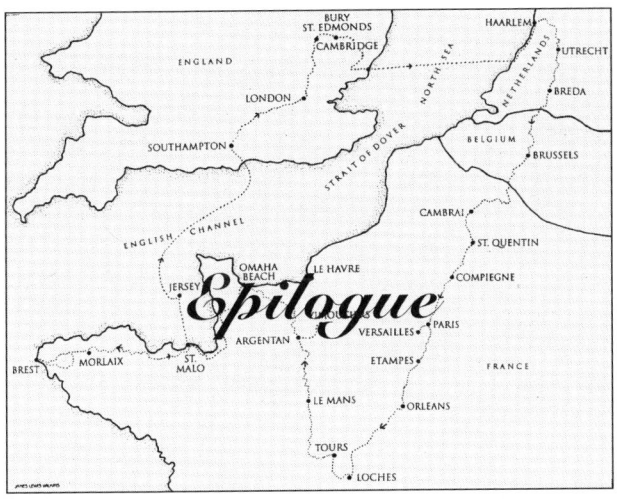

In June, 1994, while this manuscript was still in-process, Marie Alsmeyer read a letter to the editor in *The Dallas Morning News* which complained that all the historical fanfare being given to D-Day made it seem more important than it had actually been in World War II. Of course, there was quite a response from readers, including Alsmeyer, who sent in the following letter about the village of Vimoutiers:

> Let me tell you about Vimoutiers, a small village of about 2,000 persons that lay peacefully in the rolling countryside east of Caen in Normandy.
>
> When my husband and I cycled through that area in 1950, only the steeple of a magnificent old church was visible through the thick clouds. It was obvious that the center of town had been heavily bombed and streets were no longer neatly cobbled but filled with potholes and debris. Its charm was shattered and most of the town left

in rubble about 8 A.M. on June 14, 1944, eight days after D-Day.

It was purposefully and accurately bombed, but it turned out to be one of the great tragedies of war. In only 15 minutes, 250 people were killlled, hundreds wounded and incendiary bombs started fires which burned for several days, gutting most of the century-old buildings and homes.

The 9th Air Force bombed Vimoutiers because it was given information via carrier pigeons released by Germans that the village was the storage spot of large amounts of ammunition soon to be turned against the Allied Forces. This was not true, but when the truth was learned it was too late. Vimoutiers was in ruins.

In 1950, a member of the Dallas Pilot Club International asked if we could take time to visit this little village where they had donated clothes and food as well as money to rebuild the schools and hospital. We were introduced to Dr. and Mme. Boullard who had been working closely with members of the Pilot Club. She took us around the bombed-out areas. It was devastating.

"Can you imagine what it was like to attend early Mass on a peaceful Sunday morning and suddenly have the ceiling fall on you? Stained glass windows shattered all around us and when we went outside, we saw the entire village had been blown up and was in flames. Bombs would just go 'pisst' and a building would disappear."

On July 12, 1994, Marie was stunned to read another letter to the editor, this one from Phillip Boullard, living in Arlington, Texas, a *grandson* of the Mme. Boullard whom the Alsmeyers had met in Vimoutiers forty-five years before. Here is the letter:

I was stunned to read the letter from Marie Bennett Alsmeyer in Tyler about her trip to Vimoutiers, France, in 1950, where she viewed the bombing debris with Dr. and Mme. Boullard. You see, I am their grandson. I was never able to meet my grandparents because my father, in the United States during the war, met and married my

American mother, who refused to follow my father back to France. At age 13, I began a correspondence with my grandmother and my father. It was not until 1985 that I was able to take my wife and son to France to meet my father, but by then my grandmother was too ill to see me and my grandfather had passed away in 1967. I have written to the Alsmeyers and hope to set up a meeting time so that they can give me more details about this remarkable story. It is a very small world!

Index